A LIFE OF REST

God's Invitation to Step Away from Struggling,
Embrace Rest, and Flow with Your Purpose & Destiny

SUNITA AHUJA

LIFEWISE BOOKS

A LIFE OF REST
God's Invitation to Step Away from Struggling,
Embrace Rest, and Flow with Your Purpose & Destiny

Sunita Ahuja

THE HOLY BIBLE, NEW INTERNATIONAL VERSION®, NIV® Copyright © 1973, 1978, 1984, 2011 by Biblica, Inc.® Used by permission. All rights reserved worldwide.

The Holy Bible, English Standard Version (ESV) is adapted from the Revised Standard Version of the Bible, copyright Division of Christian Education of the National Council of the Churches of Christ in the U.S.A. All rights reserved.

Scripture quotation marked NKJV are taken from the New King James Version®. Copyright © 1982 by Thomas Nelson. Used by permission. All rights reserved.

Scripture quotations marked NLT are taken from the Holy Bible, New Living Translation, copyright © 1996, 2004, 2015 by Tyndale House Foundation. Used by permission of Tyndale House Publishers, Inc., Carol Stream, Illinois 60188. All rights reserved.

Scripture quotations marked TPT are from The Passion Translation®. Copyright © 2017, 2018 by Passion & Fire Ministries, Inc. Used by permission. All rights reserved. ThePassionTranslation.com.

The Christian Standard Bible. Copyright © 2017 by Holman Bible Publishers. Used by permission. Christian Standard Bible®, and CSB® are federally registered trademarks of Holman Bible Publishers, all rights reserved.

Scripture quotations marked ASV are from the American Standard Version.

Scripture quotations taken from the Amplified® Bible (AMPC), Copyright © 1954, 1958, 1962, 1964, 1965, 1987 by The Lockman Foundation. Used by permission. www.Lockman.org

Published by:

⚓LIFEWISE BOOKS
PO BOX 1072
Pinehurst, TX 77362
LifeWiseBooks.com

To contact the author: SunitaAhuja.org

ISBN (Print): 978-1-952247-17-0
ISBN (Ebook): 978-1-952247-18-7

DEDICATION

I dedicate this book to my parents who are the most wonderful human beings alive; to my loving husband who gave himself to the writing of this book by taking care of the children, running errands, and managing all things to give me the time to write; to my sweet threesome Joshua, Janae, and Joelle who are the most precious gifts in my life; and to my many friends who became guideposts during the process of me writing this book with their prayers and checking in on me...you know who you are.

CONTENTS

INTRODUCTION

This book is my calling from my Heavenly Dad and a gift to you from Him because He loves you. Perhaps more than you can imagine. But He doesn't want you to just know this; He wants to demonstrate His love to you. He wants you to know that He understands the struggles in your life from the tiniest to the largest, and He wants to be a part of these and walk alongside you to bring you out of them all.

Psalm 34:19 tells us that "the righteous person may have many troubles, but the Lord delivers him from them all."[1] His heart is to gather you up in His arms and speak words of comfort to your soul until you come to a place of calm and rest. He wants to draw you to a place of purpose, a place of fulfillment of desire, a place where your calling and creativity become one and you find the joy of living out the dreams placed in your heart by your Creator. It all starts in rest.

> Once you find that place of calm and rest where you stop struggling and your soul is settled, He is then able to draw you into this beautiful place of your divine destiny and calling for your life.

As a Christian, I have walked my Christian walk for years knowing about God's goodness and promises, yet my life seemed to be a series of struggles. There were questions, unmet needs, desperation in prayer, and some situation or the other that kept me from experiencing the fullness of what God really had for me. I was nowhere close to living a life of rest. In fact, I did not even consider it a possibility.

I had my mountaintop experiences and praise moments, but these were intermittent and hard to hold on to. It seemed that the next challenge was never too far. It seemed that I was too often in the midst of some storm with only some interspersed rest breaks. My Christian walk resembled a day at work struggling to rise and shine, a moment of stillness with morning prayers, the cup of coffee to energize the morning, the work that I sometimes was not too interested in, struggles with the team, and then a sigh of relief when it was time to pack up and leave for the day. But God doesn't call us to live this way.

Yes, we will have struggles, but our greatest victories are won when we are able to arrive at and embrace this place of rest in the midst of our struggles. As I sought Him and He sought me, He set me on a journey to understand divine rest and taught me how I can have perpetual rest in my own life.

SO, DID MY WHOLE WORLD CHANGE?

Storms still come and the waters still rise, but He has taught me how to rest in the midst of it all. He has taught me how to receive answers to my prayers and see His promises at work in my life through living this life of rest. Jesus tells us in John 16:33 that in this world we will have trouble. It almost has an element of assuredness to it. So the sooner we accept that, the better it is. However, He also tells us in the same breath, in the same verse, that He has overcome the world and He wants us to have peace in Him.

Most of us know these verses, but when storms come in our lives we don't always react with peace. Sometimes we don't know how to apply this to our lives. What does it even mean to be at rest in the midst of our unending to-do lists and obligations, in the midst of hurts and pains, difficult relationships, unfair situations, financial difficulties, and sometimes in more difficult situations like accidents, illnesses, or loss of loved ones? How can we be at rest in the midst of turmoil?

I believe God has revealed to me seven keys to unlocking a life of rest and has given me a passion to share the message of how to live and operate out of this place of rest in our lives. He showed me that His children must come to a place of stillness and rest to see His full manifestation in their lives. If we want to experience the fullness of what the Father has in store for each one of us, if we want to rise up to be everything God has called us to be and play our part in His Kingdom, we must first find this place of rest.

Through this book, you will learn how to find that place of rest in your life, and then learn how to remain in that restful place. As you do, I believe it has the potential to transform every aspect of your life. My hope and prayer is that this will set you on a path to discover your divine purpose in life and experience the very best the Father has for you!

I urge you to start this journey with me to make this "restful life" a reality for you. I pray that as you continue to read, God Himself will reveal the same truths to you and draw you into that place of unshakeable rest, as He has done for me, and bless you with His shalom.

THE JOURNEY TO
REST IN MY OWN LIFE

THE CALLING TO WRITE

For me, the call to rest and the call to write have become synonymous. Through calling me to write, God also called me out on an adventure to teach me about His rest. I remember vividly that distinct, beautiful day in the summer of 2009. We were coming home from a beach vacation. My husband was driving and our two-year-old son was napping in the back seat. I recall the conversation with my husband about feeling like God was calling me to a ministry to help propel people into a place of their divine destiny.

I had experienced recent incidents where in small yet profound ways I was able to speak to people with gentle nudges that I knew would propel them in a direction in which God wanted them to go. Right as I was talking with Him, I felt the stirring of the Holy Spirit, and it was as if God asked me to write a book that would help people to step into their divine destinies. It was an exciting moment and call for me. I immediately said, yes but I did not know the journey that lay ahead of me and all I was going to learn.

At this point, I had a full-time job as a physical therapist. Life had the regular challenges of busyness with taking the kid to daycare, working full time, and being tired. "So much to do and so little time" was the typical mantra for those years. Weekends, movies, and vacation time were the times of rest, even though they never really felt restful. There seemed to be so much work involved with even going away on a trip to the beach, and then so much work to put the umbrella up and setting things up for a little bit of time to try to laze in the sun.

The sun would be too bright and the water too cool. The kids needed to be fed, and it seemed like rest was just an illusion to covet. Hormonal imbalances, mood swings, and work challenges were the norm. The difficult colleague at work and relative in my extended family could easily wreck the mood for the day. The earlier years of marriage brought with it personality differences and marriage wars.

It certainly helped that I was a Christian, and my faith in God allowed me to sort of cast it all on Him and believe for good outcomes. However, as I look back, life was far from restful. In fact, stress and turmoil were pretty much the overriding emotion with an underlay of a rest in having a deep knowing

God was with me. But mostly, rest then meant vacations, sleep, watching TV, or lying in bed with a good book.

A THROWBACK

I remember even as a little girl I had a passion to write. I would write essays, poems, and stories. I would journal. I remember a few published poems in the local newspaper and even getting some fan mail as a young teenager. But then growing up it seems somewhere along the way I stepped away from my passion to write. It was not intentional. It just happened. I went to college to get a degree in physical therapy. Life got busy, and there was no time or even desire to write.

I went through my years of growing up and the inner challenges that come with it—the issues with self-esteem, the desire to be someone and belong, the search for my inner identity, the focus on professional growth, and the dreams about what my future would look like. This day as we drove back from the beach brought back to me the memories of the passion I had to write even as a young child. I remember how the writing would just flow, and those were the best times when I could put pen to paper and write my heart out. I had forgotten all about it, but clearly God had not. And He was calling me back to it. It was almost as if I had first needed to find my true identity in Him and fully surrender my life and calling to Him before He reinstated the thing I had been so passionate about. I was very excited about it. I had no trepidations because I knew the One who was calling me to it would be the One who would accomplish it!

I have learned and am fully persuaded that wherever we are in life, as we look to God and walk with Him, He brings us to the place He has destined for us so we can utilize the passions He has put inside of us.

We may feel like we are disconnected from our deepest life calling for a season, but in that season, God does deep work in us to prepare us for whatever He has called us to be and do. This is our place of divine alignment as God does inner and outer calibration to put us on a path we were always meant to be on. In my own life, this was certainly true as I found myself, through circumstances, leaning more and more on Him and developing a closer walk with Him. In turn, He was able to steer me and change me and my world from the inside out and then restore the purpose, passion, and calling He had destined for me.

MY GROWTH AS A CHRISTIAN

When I became a Christian, I was in my early twenties. One of the very first things that transpired with me was that I became an avid reader of the Bible. Besides this, I started to hear God's voice. I would seek out quiet places and spend long periods of time listening to God, put pen to paper, and write what He was speaking to me. I would journal for hours on end. It was as if the Bible came to life, and His Rhema Word started the process of transformation in my life. I have been journaling for years now. It has been such a joy to me to pick up my journal and seek His face for all the answers to my life's questions, big and small. Over and over I would write all my prayers, and I got such joy out of checking my prayers off as He answered them. I learned to pour out my heart and soul to Him in my journals. Not only that, I had pages of revelations regarding His nature, His Kingdom, how He wants us to live, and so much more. So on this day when He asked me to write a book, I was thrilled at the prospect of serving God through writing, my two biggest passions: God and writing, coming together.

Having walked through desert experiences where things didn't exactly go my way, as we all do, I had somehow conditioned myself to believe that God's promises were sort of out there and kept us going through this life where difficulties seem to just be part and parcel of the journey. I was conditioned to believing that I needed to bow and accept everything coming my way. When God asked me to write, the thought of being asked to do something I actually loved was almost hard for me to accept. Clearly, I did not yet fully understand God's ways. It was like an intersection where my life intersected with God's plan for my life, when I was ready to embrace it. I knew this was going to be a God thing. Clearly this was not something I had thought about or planned to do. It was going to be an act of surrender. My passion and calling were coming together to serve God in my life, and I was excited about it.

OVERCOMING CHALLENGES

Of course, I expected this to happen right away since God had spoken to me about it and commissioned me to write. So, I diligently bought a new journal and kept writing as I always had and nothing changed. I did not know what I was writing about.

My revelations seemed to be a little disconnected from each other, and I had no clue where I was going with my writing. But the commission from God never left me. I was always conscious that I was called to write, and this book He had spoken about must be written. And life continued to happen. Then in the summer of 2011, we were blessed with twin girls! It was a hard pregnancy. They were born prematurely and had to be in the neonatal intensive care unit for about a month.

God had blessed us financially, and I was able to quit my job to be home with my four-year-old son and newborn twin girls. It was a time of celebration. I had never had the luxury to be able to be away from the routine of work to be home for an extended period. In my mind, I thought it was surely the time for me to write this book God had called me to write. I tried. But it was all scattered, and I had no clue what my book was about except that it was meant to propel someone into their destiny as God intended it to be. I remember feeling much guilt over the book not being written faster. I blamed myself for not being organized enough. I thought if only I could wake up at 4:00 a.m. every morning and get more organized with my life, I could get this book written. But the project, as imminent as it seemed, was still far from completion.

Through this season, God was good and faithful as He always is, and He continued to work in me to transform me, speak with me, and give me revelation. During this season, we also discovered that one of our twins had some significant health challenges. Life was hard dealing with her constant vomiting, sickness, and inability to eat. She had surgery to have her adenoids and tonsils removed at age three. She was found to be eligible for a special education preschool and was enrolled for a short day. With all these challenges, I was unable to return to work. Family resources were drained, and the book was not yet written. When I look back, I had every reason to be anxious about our life situation and future, but I realize I walked through all of those challenges with God-given supernatural peace and rest in the midst of the storm. God was constantly teaching me His truths and walking the path with me. He was teaching me life lessons on living a restful life.

LEARNING TO REST

God was writing lessons in my heart and my mind. He was giving me revelations about His goodness, His love, His plans for people, and above all, He was teaching me the keys to living a life of "rest." God has shown me how He calls everyone to a life of rest. Through my journey, He has shown me how to make it a reality in my own life. In 2018, I put aside time and really started to write this book with help from the Launch Author Coaching program. However, the pressures of life called me back to work. With three kids in elementary school, an on-call job, a house to look after, and everything else that goes with it, it continued to be hard for me to write. Not only that, God was still doing a work in my heart and life. He continued to give me revelation and make this place of rest more and more real in my life. It was as if with every challenge I faced, there was a new place I walked in His rest. The Holy Spirit prompted me to walk a twenty-eight-day journey to rest with Him, and it was nothing short of miraculous! This time became a sacred time where I believe I had a clear vision of the seven keys to rest that I share in this book.

Finally, He has set me free to write this book. He has processed me, given me revelation, and made this happen in my own life. I can truly say I have found my place of sabbath rest, and I have learned how to make it my home, an unshakeable place that cannot be taken from me. Not because we don't have hardship or financial pressures, not that we don't have challenges with our children, not that we don't have to maintain our homes and walk through difficult relationships. But despite these things, God has shown to me truths and revealed secrets that I am excited to share. In fact, just through the process of writing this book we were bombarded with unusual and unexpected life situations, such as car theft, job loss, financial upheavals, unexpected home repairs, and sickness. These were opportunities for us to be anxious, distraught, and fearful. But God has done such wonderful work in my heart that we lived through these with praise and joy and deep rest. They became opportunities for us to see how God would lead us through a time of uncertainty to certain victory as we hung on faith, hope, and rest in Him. And true to His Word, the Lord has brought us out of all these and continues to do so in amazing ways as only He can!

2

WHAT DOES THE BIBLE SAY ABOUT REST?

LIFE BEFORE REST

I remember when faith was not the driving force in my life. It seemed as if the ceiling to living was palpable and low. The bumps on the road of life and jars from the walls and ceiling seemed to constantly limit and were hard on the mind, body, and emotions. Hope was based on the finite and temporal. Even in the midst of the good situations, there was an often urge to escape. Instead of fully engaging with what was within reach, there was the propensity to disengage and find something more meaningful, or just more. But then with the entry of faith and relationship with God, the ceiling seemed to just lift off, and all of a sudden there were enormous possibilities. It was confusing to the mind that still needed to orient to the new, but there was no escaping that the finite was now linked to the infinite. Hope now became the certainty of a belief in a real person. There was the urge now to dig deep within and engage with what was around to seek out directions and paths as never before. So, was life not good before the entry of faith? Can we have good lives without faith?

We can work hard and create fairly good lives for ourselves. We can continue to live and work out of our finite potential and resources; however, I believe deep in our hearts we all long for a sense of wholeness or shalom in our lives. The feeling that we can get more out of our lives can cause us to strive and struggle for more and leave us tired. Even our Christian lives can be a struggle. We know about God's love and goodness, but we don't experience the full manifestation of everything God wants to be to us and has for us. Thankfully, we don't have to live that way. No matter where you are in life today, there is a restful place that the Almighty has for you out of which flow all things. In fact, our very strength and striving can actually hinder us from the very best our heavenly Father has for us.

In this world, we receive all things by striving, but in the Kingdom of God, we receive all things through rest.

THE LITERAL MEANING OF REST

The Hebrew word for rest is *nuach*,[1] which means "to settle down or to be quiet." Oftentimes, we think of biblical rest as the sabbath from the Hebrew word *Shabbat*, which means "to rest from labor."[2] The Greek word for rest is *anapauó* meaning "to give intermission from labor, by implication refresh."[3] Some of my favorite translations of rest are appeased, calm, free, give comfort, let go, put aside, remain, rid themselves, satisfy, settle, and wait quietly. In addition to these, the ones I love from the *Strong's Exhaustive Concordance* that truly bring out the essence of the word are "to remain, to dwell."[4] Let's put these words in the context of our souls. If the soul is our being—the mind and emotions—imagine a soul that is settled, quiet, comforted, calm, and free. Imagine a soul that is able to let go, that is refreshed and satisfied and able to dwell and remain in this place. A soul that experiences all, yet is at rest.

This is not the typical experience for most. Rest seems to be such an elusive and transient phase in most people's lives. We are conditioned to believing that rest is synonymous with inactivity. For many, rest means finally being able to sit in their recliner and get that fav television program going. Or going away on vacation. There are so many interruptions to rest. We are tired from our jobs, relationships, financial pressures, and just the daily grind. What happens when there are unexpected injuries, illnesses, expenses, or traumatic events in our lives? None is immune from these. These things can turn our minds into battlefields, and our emotions can be all over the place.

Unrest can cause people to go into downward spirals or indulge in questionable stuff people do to get some peace, equanimity, equilibrium, and respite from life. Many sicknesses and diseases are directly caused by this unrestful state or stress. A majority of us accept this as part of life and are tossed by the winds that come our way. Even for Christians who have surrendered their lives to Christ, life can be a series of ups and downs with occasional glimpses of God's goodness and phases of rest from spiritual battles. Surely, we can't possibly expect to have perpetual rest in our lives? What kind of a rest does God offer us?

REST—IN THE BEGINNING

God has always meant for us to have a life of rest. In order to get there, we must first be fully convinced that this is God's will for us. Without that conviction, it will be impossible for us to get there. Second, we must understand what rest means according to the Bible. Let's take a closer look at the rest God calls us to. There are many scripture references that point us to a life free from worry and anxiety, and we are asked to cast our cares on the Lord. In our day-to-day lives, it is very important that we live this way. But through my journey to find rest, the Holy Spirit has highlighted to me the enormity of the call to "God's rest" right from the beginning of creation in the chapter of Genesis. Let's look at the origin of God's rest in the Bible.

The Bible tells us that once the work of creation was finished, God "rested from all his work" (Genesis 2:2, NIV). It was done, and it was all good. It was time to enjoy the perfection of creation. Prior to creating mankind, God had already created light, day and night—or time as we know it—the sky, earth, dry land, the seas and all vegetation, all planetary bodies, fish, birds of the air, and all other living creatures living on land. And He pronounced each of these "very good" (Genesis 1:31, NIV).

The creation around mankind was perfect. Man was placed in this finished, perfect creation. He did not work to make it happen. Mankind entered into "God's rest." But not only was he to enjoy God's finished, perfect creation that was "very good" but also given a charge to rule and reign over God's creation. He was given the work of tending to the Garden of Eden where all provision was given. This was meant to be man's life of rest. It is clear that God did not create man so he would somehow make it through life, toiling and struggling to make ends meet. In man's assignment in the Garden of Eden was his life's calling to rule over and care for creation along with God. But we see that this did not last long. Once Adam and Eve ate from the tree of knowledge of good and evil and chose death instead of life, everything changed.

THE ROOT OF UNREST

God created mankind to be the highest of His creation. The one to whom all dominion is given to rule over the rest of His magnificent creation. And along with that, He gives us intelligence and a will. He chose not to create weak beings controlled by His power but intelligent beings with the ability to exercise all of our potential. Life and death are set before us, and we are given a choice. A choice that can lead to very opposing results. Clearly, man was created with identity. He had potential, a purpose, and a charge along with moral boundaries for his good. Once man ate from the tree of knowledge of good and evil everything changed. The atmosphere shifted instantly. Man felt shame for the first time, then he blamed Eve for the act, and then there was the pain of being driven out of Eden to a life of toil and labor.

Due to Adam and Eve choosing to eat from the tree of knowledge of good and evil, which they foreknew would bring them death over the tree of life, they were banished from Eden and their right to eat from the tree of life was removed from them so they would not live in this sinful state forever. Once out of Eden, they were separated from a life of dominion, blessings, and provision to a life of painful toil for daily bread (Genesis 3:17). Because of their wrong choice, the ground was cursed and produced thorns and thistles (Genesis 3:18). In this world, now they were to have troubles (John 16:33) due to the manifestation of sin.

A world that was meant to be delightful would now be difficult. It was as if there was instant separation from indescribable glory and rest to a life of painful toil. Where everything was provided in the Garden of Eden and man was to tend to it and guard it, now he was to earn his daily bread by the sweat of his brow in a land that would also produce thorns and thistles. He lost access to the tree of life. Shame, blame, and pain emerged very quickly as the chief byproducts of the eating of the knowledge of good and evil versus eating from the tree of life.

GOD'S PROMISE OF REST

Let's fast forward to the New Testament and look at chapters 3 and 4 of Hebrews. Hebrews 3 references the Israelites during the time Moses led them out of Egypt. Despite God's deliverance from Egypt, His promises, and the manifestation of many miracles, their unbelief and sin caused them to go astray and many perished in the wilderness, even though God had promised them a land. For those who disobeyed, God swore that they would never enter His rest (Hebrews 3:18, paraphrased). So, we see that they were not able to enter because of their disobedience and unbelief. Hebrews 4:1 (NIV) tells us that "the promise of entering his rest still stands" and then urges us to "be careful that none of you be found to have fallen short of it." Hebrews 4:9 (NIV) says, "There remains, then, a Sabbath-rest for the people of God." Hebrews 4:10 (NIV) tells us that means, "for anyone who enters God's rest also rests from their works, just as God did from his." Hebrews 4:11 (NIV) follows by urging us to "therefore, make every effort to enter that rest." This verse has intrigued me and has now become my pathway to living a life of rest. It is paradoxical but sums up so beautifully what God desires for us. He wants us to cease from our struggling and striving.

God's desire for us is not to live a life of strife but rather to strive only to enter into His rest.

What does this mean to us today? The rest that was promised to the Israelites that they did not appropriate, due to their unbelief and disobedience, now still remains for you and me. We are invited into the "promise of rest." But God does not do anything outside of our will. All His promises to us are invitations. We believe His promises and appropriate them by faith. We must engage with His promise of rest. To the Israelites under the leadership of Moses, this was a literal land. It encompassed their deliverance from Egypt and the manifestation of many miracles for their provision along with the expectation to follow the commandments given to them so they could arrive at their destined land of Canaan, God's promised land, a land flowing with milk and honey. This is where they were to be fruitful and multiply and be blessed of the Lord. Similarly, we all have our Canaan we must get to, our promised land of rest.

REST IN RETURNING TO GOD'S ORIGINAL INTENT

As much as God banished Adam and Eve from the Garden of Eden and from eating of the tree of the knowledge of good and evil, because He did not want them to live forever in that sinful state, God's intention for mankind never changed. Through history, with everything God has done and continues to do, His intention for mankind remains the same. He wants us to recover our identities that were lost in our separation from Him. He wants us to know who we are through establishing relationship and partnering with Him. He wants us to understand the potential He has put inside each one of us.

The Almighty continues to invite us to receive and accept our original blueprints, and as we partner in our restored relationship with Him, we are to rise up to be everything we are called to be. For those who have accepted this invitation, He invites us to rise up and take authority over His creation. He wants us to rule and reign. Creation is waiting for the sons and daughters of the Almighty Creator to break off the shackles of false identity, to take ownership of who He has created us to be and embrace our destinies, and to take back what has been lost and restore to the world the original intent of God. "Creation waits in eager expectation for the children of God to be revealed" (Romans 8:19, NIV). God's desire is to see creation being "liberated from its bondage to decay and brought into the freedom and glory of the children of God" (Romans 8:21, NIV).

Only when we enter into our true identities as sons and daughters of God, created in His image and carrying His glory, can our prayer for His Kingdom to come and His will to be done on earth as it is in Heaven become a reality. God intends for Heaven to invade the earth through us, and we need to be ready to play our part.

THE WAY

In sending Jesus and the reconciliation with the Father that was offered to us through His life, death, and resurrection, today we have the pathway "to enter that rest" (Hebrews 4:11, NIV) available to us. This rest is based on the finished work of Christ, just like the rest of God when He finished the work of creation. When Jesus died on the cross, His last words were "It is finished"

(John 19:30, NIV). The work had been done, the path had been laid. We are invited to enter into our promised lands, to enter into our Eden, to enter into God's rest by following Christ. We are then again worthy of fulfilling God's original intention. Once again, we are not sinful in His eyes. We are justified. He sees us blameless. The Bible tells us that "As he is so also are we in this world" (1 John 4:17, ESV). He proclaims us sons and daughters.

In doing so, we are once again entrusted with access to the tree of life and also the tree of knowledge of good and evil. I believe the charge is still the same. We are to take back the dominion that was initially given to us that we gave away. We are to rule and reign. We are to take back the charge to tend to the Garden of Eden, the garden of delight. God Himself put hope in that "creation itself will be liberated from its bondage to decay and brought into the freedom and glory of the children of God," (Romans 8:21, NIV) of whom Christ was the forerunner. We are again pleasing to Him. He looks at us and says "very good." We are meant to eat from the tree of life for perpetual life versus the tree of knowledge of good and evil, which only brings death in our thoughts, feelings, words, and actions.

REST VS. INACTIVITY

Obviously, God did not create us to have the sit-on-a-couch-and-watch-TV kind of rest. There is a place for the sabbath rest, the seventh day rest. That is one of the keys to a restful living. However, we are promised "God's rest" (Hebrews 4:10, NIV) perpetually. We are invited into His rest through our faith and obedience. This rest is not a place of inactivity but a place where we "tend and keep" (Genesis 2:15, NKJV) the Garden of Eden out of a place of rest, not a place of striving. In the original Garden of Eden, all provision was given, and everything was good. Everything was blessed—time, provision, and ability. There was no anxious striving. Just a charge.

Imagine the joy of having dominion with no anxious caring, striving, or shortcomings. God gives to each of us this delightful Eden or realm of influence. He gives us what it takes to tend and keep our Edens. He gives us the potential or creativity and resources we need to rule our gardens. That is the kind of restful life our Creator meant for you to live. And His intention for us today is the same. Oftentimes, we just don't recognize this or are not diligent to take care of our gardens and be patient to wait on the blessings and overflow that is promised.

> We are meant to live restful lives, not by being inactive, but in knowing who we are, in utilizing our gifts and talents, in knowing what our charge is in our areas of influence, in exercising authority to be world changers in these areas, in remaining connected to the bread of life, and in turn, being blessed of God and being fruitful and multiplying in every area of our lives.

I believe Heaven will be just like this, a beautiful place where we engage our creative talents forever with no sense of striving, a life of perfect harmony and rest. Again, we are to make that choice. Will we believe? Will we choose life? Will we honor the boundaries He lays down for us? Will we enter into His rest?

3
LIFE, CREATIVITY AND REST

OUR UNIQUE, DIVINE PATH

We are all given a garden, our land to occupy. Our Edens are meant to be delightful. Our Edens are meant to give us pleasure. Our gardens are our domains, where we plow, till, guard and take care of what's given to us. We are given the resources and potential to take care of our gardens and to rule over this land. This is our God-ordained divine destiny. We all have gifts and talents that help us engage in our destinies. Within this land, I am convinced that we are all meant to be highly creative.

We can only be truly satisfied when we discover and utilize our gifts to become the highly creative people that rule over our domains as we are destined to.

Then, not only are we fulfilled, but we also generate resources and are able to contribute to the world the way we were all meant to. We are positioned to fulfill our purposes and destinies. As we start to walk out our destinies, we start to partner with the Almighty to bring about His good purpose for this world within each one of our realms of influence.

For people whose relationship with the Almighty is not yet restored, they can feel lost in the maze of life with its complexities. Their paradigm of life is limited to their temporal, physical world. At best, they can rely on themselves, do the best they can, and enjoy what life offers them. Even Christians who have restored relationships with the Almighty can still feel lost until their lives start to intersect with their divinely ordained paths. Once our relationship with the Almighty is restored, there is a path that opens up to us to fully restore us, and we are transformed so we can truly become who we are created to be. The pathway is also opened up to restore our lives to where they were meant to go. This is the beginning of the restful lives God wants us to have.

The Word of God in Psalm 139:16 tells us that all the days ordained for us are written in His book before one of them came to be. Also, in Ephesians 2:10, we are told that we are God's handiwork, created in Christ Jesus to do good works, which God prepared in advance for us to do. Clearly, we are created to pursue our deepest calling, that which is ordained for us by God Himself. It is a part of our blueprint and DNA. And it is not enough for us to just know this. We must find our way there. We must not only be, but know and feel that we are in the heart and center of where we are meant to be in life.

We can only be at rest when we start to flow with our unique, individual, divine destinies.

OUR GIFTS AND TALENTS

During the journey of our lives, as much as God is on our side and does everything to keep us on the path of our destinies, there is the enemy who also does everything he can "to steal and kill and destroy" (John 10:10, NIV). There is a very real battle, not only for our souls but once we have reconciled with God, then to keep us on the path of our divinely destined paths in life. We are all unique, and God has put destiny and purpose in each one of us. We all have God-given talents that we are meant to discover and put to use. Each one of our lives is meant to have an impact on this world. In Matthew 25:14–30, in the parable of the talents, Jesus describes what we are to do with the talents given to us. He describes this in talking about what "the kingdom of heaven will be like…" (Matthew 25:1, NIV).

It is interesting that Jesus makes such a strong connection between us using the talents given to us, bearing fruit, and multiplication to what the Kingdom of Heaven will look like. In the parable, He goes on to describe what happens to the one who has been given five talents by his master, the one who has been given four talents, and the one who has been given one talent. The one who has five talents works hard, multiplies, and now has double, and the one who has four talents does the same. But the one who has one talent buries it and does nothing about it.

We all have God-given gifts in us. There are those who are called to preach or be missionaries. There are those who are meant to be musicians and lead worship. There are those who are meant to be business people, bankers, doctors, teachers, or stay-at-home moms. Within our gardens, we are to fully engage with our talents and produce more. This is where we are blessed and multiply. This is where we rule and reign. This is the place from which we impact the world with the Kingdom of God. As we engage with our talents and create, we have resources. As we become highly creative, and our talents multiply, we start to flow with our divine destinies. In the parable of the talents, when the master returns and sees the multiplication in the lives of the first two servants, He sets them over more responsibilities and invites them to enter into His joy (Matthew 25:21). The one who neglects to do anything about the talent given to him loses what he has and eventually loses all experience of the Kingdom of Heaven. It is the same with us today. As we discover our gifts and utilize them, we multiply, and we are given more influence and authority in our realms. Not only are we impacted, but we expand the Kingdom of God. And in this, there is great joy in our lives. This is what the Kingdom of Heaven looks like!

Then, we are no more lost and trying to find our way in life. This is a place where we are fully awake and fully alive, fully creative, fully utilizing our gifts, fully engaged with our destinies, and fully at rest as we reverberate with the heartbeat of God, with the frequencies of Heaven. In this place, even as we are deeply and passionately hungry for more, we are totally and completely rested in the arms of a God who passionately loves us. This is a place where our souls are settled, a place where we know our needs will always be met because we know our Father knows what we need before we ask him (Matthew 6:8). This is the place where we are blessed by God, and we can be fruitful and multiply. We know who we are and what our calling is. We are not confused, and our prayers are not desperate. We are partnering with God to become who we are called to be, do what we are called to do, and are on our way to becoming world changers.

ABUNDANT LIVES

God created man in His image, intelligent and free. But He has always intended for us to choose life over death and made provision for it. In the Garden of Eden, God made available to the first man the tree of life and also the tree of knowledge of good and evil. Man was informed that the eternal consequence of partaking from the tree of knowledge of good and evil would be death. Clearly, man was to choose the fruit of the tree of life for eternal life versus death. We know that man did not believe God and rather believed that something was being withheld from him. In disobedience and lack of faith, he embraced sin and lost access to the tree of life. For generations, God looked for those whose hearts had the willingness to hear Him and follow through with His plans in order to redeem mankind from the curse of sin and death. We see the lives of many in the Old Testament interspersed with God's promises, His leading, His presence, and His promises, and yet due to the disobedience of man and his embracing of sin, redemption of mankind to God's original plan has been a sure but slow process.

A radical shift happens when Jesus, who was the Word, came in the form of a man to live a sinless life and then give His life up as a sin offering for mankind. In doing so, we are brought face-to-face with a choice. Will we choose life or death? In accepting the sacrifice of Jesus, not only do we receive God's forgiveness and are reconciled with Him, but in John 6:35, NIV, "Jesus declared, 'I am the bread of life. Whoever comes to me will never go hungry, and whoever believes in me will never be thirsty.'" In following Jesus, who is also the bread of eternal life, we are not only to inherit eternal life but in partaking from the bread of life we are not to be hungry or thirsty right here on this earth. We are to be fully satisfied. We are to be connected to the source of life for our constant replenishment. What was lost due to the first man, Adam, has now been restored through Jesus, the last Adam. Roman 5:17, NIV says "For if, by the trespass of the one man, death reigned through that one man, how much more will those who receive God's abundant provision of grace and of the gift of righteousness reign in life through the one man, Jesus Christ!" We are to take back the mandate that was given to the first man to rule and reign over God's creation.

We can do this wherever we are in life today. God did not just give us the gift of life and then expect us to make something out of it. I think our Creator knew we were going to make mistakes along the way and made all provision for us. We all, without exception, also have hurts and pains from our pasts. This tangible life that flows from the heart of the Creator has the ability to wipe away the baggage of the past from our souls, the wrongs we have done, and the wrongs that have been done to us. A divine exchange is available to all. A new life for our old. Not only do we have a fresh chance at life, not only does it wipe away all negative baggage, but it also contains everything we need to write a better future—divine wisdom, guidance, favor, and so much more. In partaking of the bread of life, we have a way to receive of His very own fresh, new life continuously.

Daily and even moment by moment as we hook up to His great reservoir, we receive a fresh supply. A refueling of life. The Creator is able to partner with us, which has always been His plan. As we partake of His life in exchange for ours, as we are transformed into His original intention for us, creativity in us begins to blossom with His own life as the element of it that transforms us from the inside out. The abundant life that only God can give us removes all shackles and hindrances within us that block us from being the creative genius each one of us is called to be in our giftings and callings. And as we continue to feed on His very life, we flourish and our gardens flourish. We have the potential to become world changers. The choice is ours. How far do we want to go in our journey with God?

LIFE BIRTHS CREATIVITY

As we continue the process of transformation, we become highly creative moms, teachers, athletes, musicians, or whatever we are called to be. Only when we live this way can we be truly joyful, satisfied, and impact the world. We are partnering with the Creator and taking care of our Edens. We are blessed, we bear fruit, and multiply. When we operate out of this place, provision and resources become available to us to do what the maker has called us to do. Our rest comes from being fully grafted into God's purposes for us, which are very good and blessed. There is no striving for goals but a sense of rest or abiding in Him. We are not striving; we are one with the heartbeat of the Almighty. We are the chord that is moving in perfect unison with the Creator's intent for us. This is the kind of restful living our Creator calls us to.

Many find their gifts and talents and are even able to use them well. Not all artists, humanitarian workers, and scientists know God. But they are able to use these talents in natural, finite ways. What happens when we are able to use these with the Spirit of God breathing on us? Our natural talents take on a supernatural element, and our experiences are transformed to heights that we could not possibly conceive in the natural realm. By ourselves, we are frail and tire easily.

It is a well-known fact that some of history's biggest thinkers and most creative people had issues with mental health.[1] Charles Dickens, the famous author, suffered from severe bouts of depression. Charles Darwin, the father of the theory of evolution, suffered from such a severe form of agoraphobia that he was not even able to interact with his own children. Winston Churchill had bipolar disorder, and Abraham Lincoln suffered from depression. Ludwig van Beethoven suffered from bipolar disorder with suicidal thoughts. Vincent van Gogh is speculated to have suffered from bipolar or schizophrenia.[2] What if these world contributors with exceptional creative geniuses had hooked their creativity to God's and found their calling and purpose in the expanse of the bigger picture of God's purpose in their lives? What if they had discovered access to the bread of life and the secret to abundant life? I am certain their lives would have been happier, and their contributions to the world would have also brought them great joy!

> In using our creativity for God, we are able to refuel from an unlimited reservoir of life out of which flows the infinite creativity of the Creator Himself, and instead of painful toil, we have the restful manifestation of doing what He wants to do in this world through us. This is the place where His divine calling and our creativity become one.

The creative gifts put inside us by God are fully utilized and become our service to Him. For example, a baker may bake each cake as if he is baking it for the Lord. As he combines his natural talent with God's supernatural strategies and ideas, and works his love into his work and his customers, there is no doubt that becomes his platform to dwell in His promised land flowing with milk and honey, His promised rest. His creativity and God's calling have become one. He gains a platform to preach the Good News of the Gospel and manifest Christ. His garden of delight becomes the source of his resources. His work is blessed, and he can be fruitful and multiply in his calling. This is a type and shadow of Heaven. He might be one of the bakers baking at the marriage supper of the lamb. In this man's life, "Your kingdom come, your will be done, on earth as it is in heaven" (Matthew 6:10, NIV) becomes a reality.

In my life, my Garden is my marriage, my children, my home, and my vocation as a physical therapist. As I have walked with Jesus, my marriage has gone on from being rocky to a beautiful garden where we are the best of friends and enjoy each other. My children are my joy, pride, and enjoyment. My work is a peaceful garden where I plough, share the love and healing power of Christ, and gather my resources. My home is a place where God's presence is manifest; it's my place of literal rest. Out of my relationship with Christ and His love for me and mine for Him, I serve in the prayer ministry at church where it is my joy to pray over people, I also lead a small group at my home. Out of my relationship with God has birthed this ministry of rest. In helping even a few to find their restful place in life, I become a world changer. My creativity is fully utilized, and as I feed on God's Word and His life, as much as I am passionate for more, I am fully satisfied.

What gifts has God placed inside you? What sphere of influence has been given to you? Whether you are a stay-at-home mom or an evangelist, today you have a garden to work in.

THE CREATIVITY AND REST CONNECTION

Once we have established our relationship with our Creator by receiving the mercy He offers us in accepting the ultimate sacrifice paid for us for every possible bad thing that entered the world through the fall of mankind, we are set free to follow Him. To hear His voice. We become privileged sons and daughters of the most-High God. All His blessings are for us. He Himself has always been for us, but now we know Him and we understand what that means. He has always been present with us. But now we know His presence and can engage with Him. We can receive from Him, and not only that, we can minister to His heart by becoming people who use our gifts and callings to delight Him and bring His Kingdom here on earth. Did you know you were so important to Him that you can actually do that? It is not for some special category of people. Each one of is invited to participate. As we accept that invitation and start to live life with Him as our inner guide and compass, we start to become transformed and our gifts start to flow as never before. We are fully accepted, we are fully loved, we are confident of our provision, and our future is secure. Our creativity flows out of this place of rest. We become tools in the hands of our Maker. He delights to write a unique story in and through our lives.

As we live our lives out of His abundance, our gifts and talents become an expression of a higher calling.

HOW DO WE REST IN THE MIDDLE OF CHAOS?

HOW DO WE REST WHEN TROUBLE COMES?

In this life, trouble will come with or without notice. In John 16:33, NIV, Jesus tells His disciples, "I have told you these things, so that in me you may have peace. In this world, you will have trouble. But take heart! I have overcome the world." There is an assuredness in Jesus's words as He talks with His disciples that in this world they would have trouble. The same applies to us today. Let's face it; we live in a world where God's original intent was not fulfilled. Mankind caved to sin and did not take dominion over creation. The battle between good and evil had begun, and thousands of years later still continues. And we are given a choice to pursue life or death. In the same breath, however, Jesus also assured His disciples that He had overcome the world, and He wanted them to be at peace. He was trying to tell them that their world was not going to be perfect but they need not worry, they need not be anxious because He had paved a path they were to follow. And even today, in the midst of a difficult world and our difficult circumstances, we are to follow Him on the path He shows us.

We also know that our "enemy the devil prowls around like a roaring lion looking for someone to devour" (1 Peter 5:8, NIV). Talking about the same enemy, in John 10:10, NIV, Jesus says, "The thief comes only to steal and kill and destroy; I have come that they may have life, and have it to the full." As much as the dark side is interested in us surrendering our souls to its eternal perdition, everything God does is not only to save our souls but bring us back to that place where we pick ourselves up and partner with God as He restores us and enables us to "tend and keep" (Genesis 2:15, NKJV) our Gardens. He wants to restore our souls to His original blueprint for us without the baggage of pain, shame, and blame. He wants to restore rest to our souls, whether we are tired from running with sin, painful relationships, the challenges of sickness and disease, or just the stress and pressure of living day-to-day lives with all its demands.

What happens when trouble, sickness, and other pressures of life come knocking at the door? How do we respond? Do we cave in to it and spend our days and nights caught up in the web of the troubles of life, experiencing limitations of time, money, health, and stress? Once our minds are wrapped around our problems, or even in using all our resources believing for a resolution to the problem, we become ineffective in who we are and called to be. Even those who believe and have surrendered their lives to Christ can get swept away or distracted from their place of destiny and rest. It is a highly effective strategy of the dark side that has no real power over us, except in our minds as we begin to partner with dark thoughts that can then translate into our lives as we start to act on them, robbing us of all we are called to be through God and the manifestation of all of His promises for us.

For example, as Christians when we encounter an issue with a relationship that upsets our emotions a great deal, we can spend our time in turmoil, talking with others about it, praying, and then seeking everything in our power for a quick resolution. What if the resolution to this takes longer? Are we able to be at such rest that we can continue to partner with God's plan for us daily and be fully effective until a resolution comes? Or do we allow the enemy to steal that time and our daily destiny while we wait on the bigger issue to be resolved?

WHO WILL WE PARTNER WITH?

We can choose to do this life in our own strength. We can live the way we want, believe what we want, and reap the consequences of our choices in this world and beyond. We can also partner with the dark side and open our lives and souls to an eternity with the darkness we choose to partner with. For Christians, there is a restored relationship with God as our Father and the certainty of eternal life with Him in an eternal world called

Heaven. We can be content in that and carry on living in our strength and continue to reap the consequences of our choices. But there is so much more available to us. God calls us to so much more. All of what He offers are invitations that we choose to partner with through His Holy Spirit. We must learn how to so we can become everything God desires us to be. God is ever present, ever moving, ever acting, and ever speaking into our lives. And we must learn to hear His voice and move with the nudges of the Holy Spirit.

Today, in our lives, when the going gets tough and we feel the pain of it, what do we do? We can rely on the things we have believed in or look for something we can believe in to lessen the pain. We can rely on family and friends. If we have none, we can go the extent of relying on stuff that numbs our pain, even though temporarily, such as alcohol/ drugs/prescription medications. As Christians, we may pray, fast, or get Christian counseling, and all these are good. But what do we do until the answer comes? What do we do while we are still in the midst of a painful situation? What do we do while we are waiting? What if your soul is bombarded with pain? What if the situation around you is unfair, things are out of order, and things need to be fixed? When faced with challenges, do we in some way try to change our circumstances; change people around us; pray for God to change our circumstances; or do our best to change, shift, and move things until we feel better? Even our prayers can be prayers to shift this or that. I believe these situations have great power to propel us into something greater. We know "And we know that all things work together for good to those who love God, to those who are called according to His purpose" (Romans 8:28, NKJV).

Can we rest in that and continue to remain at the heart and center of His will for us daily and continue to fulfil His calling in our lives through these difficult times? Can we continue to rest as we abide in Him?

INVITATION TO REST

This is your moment of invitation, your moment to do the thing that might be hardest. In the midst of our souls wanting to run to fix whatever might be wrong, accept the invitation to enter into God's rest. Have faith in Him, follow the path He shows you, and be diligent not to cross over the boundaries He places in your life. Rest in knowing that He will bring you out of bondage, rest in knowing that He will fight the battle for you, rest in knowing that He will make the way, rest in knowing that He will have the last word, and rest in knowing that you inherit your land through faith and in following the path He shows you. Literally, rest your weary soul until it feels the longings of God, until it feels God's embrace, until it hears God's voice again. Rest until you feel loved and comforted by God. Rest until you are able to believe that God is on your side, until your mind and heart are able to believe all of His promises for you in that situation. Rest in His embrace. It is a gift, not something you have to earn or deserve. That is the Good News of the Gospel.

God has made a way. He placed Adam in the Garden of Eden, which also means "delight." He promised a land of rest to the Israelites. It doesn't matter if you are at fault and have brought bad stuff on yourself. It doesn't matter how bad things around you look. None of it matters except that you turn it over to Him and then allow your soul to rest. There is nothing God cannot do if you can turn it over to Him and allow Him room to come through. That does not mean we do nothing. It just means that we choose to first be still and know that He is God (Psalm 46:10). We first cast all our anxiety on Him (1 Peter 5:7). We "seek first his kingdom and his righteousness" (Matthew 6:33, NIV). We must first enter the place of rest. Then we move as He illuminates the path for us and we know clearly what we are to do, which way we are to go.

Today, be intentional in partnering with His spirit and engaging with your circumstances to bring about His Kingdom in your life. Partner with the Holy Spirit to manifest the fruits of the Spirit. Even if your life situation, work situation, relationships, or financial situation seems hopeless and you don't see even a ray of light, you still have a garden to tend and keep. That garden then is within you; it is in your heart and spirit. Work on the garden inside of you to cultivate love, peace, and joy. As you continue to partner with the Holy Spirit and seek to manifest His Kingdom, it will spill into your situation and start to change it. If you find yourself in the wrong place in life, once you see where you need to be going, follow the path that opens up to you. Engage with the Holy Spirit, engage with God's promises in your life. Follow the path that brings life. Be radical. Guard your heart, your thoughts, your emotions, and actions. Do not let seeds of unforgiveness, unbelief, and disobedience take root in your heart.

Let His rest reign in your heart until you become a carrier of His rest.

OUR DAY-TO-DAY LIVES

We must learn to rest in the midst of all we do with no anxious striving. We must rest in the knowledge of who we are, what our purpose is, what our gifts and callings are, and actively engage with our destinies. How do we apply this to our daily lives? What does it mean to eat from the tree of life versus the tree of knowledge of good and evil? What does it mean to eat the "bread of life" (John 6:35, NIV)? I have learned that I make this choice through the process of making daily choices in everything I think, speak, and do. I ask myself, in doing so, who am I partnering with? Life or death? Rest or unrest? When we partner with life, it always brings rest.

I have found that in every choice you make, you either choose life or death. It is a radical way to live but so worth it. Let's start with your morning cup of coffee. What are your first thoughts when you wake up? Are you thinking of the most pressing things for the day? The things that must be done, the things that are wrong and must be fixed, the bad stuff that happened the previous day, shortages of time and money? Do you then let these things propel you into the day until you are drained and need some rest in the form of whatever rest is for you? I believe a lot of us live our lives that way. Even Christians can pray and then carry on with their lives hoping and praying that somewhere God will intervene, help, and bless.

Let's reverse this scenario. Let's go back to your waking moment and see how you can partner with the Spirit of life, which brings peace and rest. What if you were to choose to eat from the tree of life and remind yourself that you are blessed, your time is blessed, that this day you will utilize your creative gifts, and live in the garden of delight no matter what attacks come your way, no matter how your situation looks? I have done this over and over and found that bad things will happen, but that doesn't change how I live, the choices I make, and the resulting life of peace and rest. After all, God has promised us that when we delight in Him, He will give us the desires of our heart (Psalm 37:4).

When bad things happen, when you don't know what to do, and when life doesn't meet up to your dreams, the best thing you can do is rest. Rest in His Word, His promises, and in His sweet presence, which has everything you need. I believe that with all my heart; God has shown this to be true over and over again in my life.

Rest is the key for us to attain all of His wonderful promises and victory in all things.

MAKE THE BEAUTIFUL PLACE CALLED
REST YOUR HOME

This rest is a beautiful place. This is where God finally becomes the God of our lives. This is where we encounter God, the good, good Father, and Friend. This is where we are still enough to hear His voice that calms our fears. In Psalm 46:10, God invites us to be still and know that He is God. What does this mean? Do we not do anything? Do we just sit down and become inactive in the middle of challenges thrown at us in life? I believe that as we are going through situations, if we can get to the restful place in our soul and keep our minds and our eyes on Him long enough, we start to hear His voice, we start to see what He is doing in our situation, and we start to experience His goodness in the midst of difficult situations. This is where meaningful exchanges and transactions happen between us and His Kingdom. This is where the river of life is able to refresh us. This is where we receive revelation from Him. This is where we receive direction and guidance. This is where God's thoughts and ideas permeate us. This is where we start to recognize heavenly encounters, dreams, and visions. As we stay in this place, this is where we start to recognize the Father's heartbeat and start to reverberate with it. This is where our struggles, even to be good Christians, end. This is the point of surrender where we finally are one with God, and we think what God thinks, do what God wants us to do, and we can rest in knowing that His will is being done in our lives. This must be the starting point of our Christian lives. This is the foundation we must build on. Knowing God needs nothing from us. There is nothing we can do to please God or serve Him outside of this place.

5 KEYS TO REST

I hope that in seeing God's intention and invitation for us to enter His rest, we are convinced that it is God's desire that we live restful lives and understand what rest is according to God's plan. I hope this changes the paradigm of rest we typically have, which is seeing it as a time of inactivity, a time where we can sit back or disengage from life. We are called to be at rest in the midst of everything life brings our way and in the midst of everything we do. We cannot find true rest for our souls until we fully engage with our destinies in our individual unique most highly creative way. Until we get there, rest remains an elusive entity we attempt to find by disengaging from life. Rest should not be an elusive entity that we cannot have. Rest is achievable. We must learn to walk this out in our lives. It is within our reach. God urges us to "make every effort to enter that rest" (Hebrews 4:11, NIV). This rest is the key to living out our destinies and fulfilling everything God has created us to be and do.

First, we must be radical in our walk with God. We must be all in. There is no way for us to receive all of what our heavenly Father has for us unless we are willing to step fully into accepting everything He has for us. The Bible is a book of invitations. God does not overrule our will. He invites us, He woos us with His love, and He opens our spiritual faculties. He may direct us through people and circumstances, but in the end, it is up to us to accept and partner with everything He has for us. We cannot expect to see His work in our lives unless we are willing to step back and allow Him to come through for us. We must say yes, and this yes is not a one-time thing. Of course, there is the one-time yes to accepting the sacrifice of Jesus to restore our relationship with the Father, but then there is the daily yes in everything in our lives. We must partner with the Holy Spirit and the Kingdom of God in our thinking, in our speaking, and in our actions. We must learn to flow with His Spirit.

I believe the Holy Spirit has illuminated to me seven areas as keys that can help us live restful lives. All of these work harmoniously in our lives to keep us in the wonderful place of rest. In my own life, If I find myself at unrest, I use these keys to check which of these areas is causing me unrest and then partner with the Holy Spirit in that area to recover my restful place. I pray that as you dig into the seven keys, they will bless you and you will start to identify areas of unrest in your own lives and see a shift as you engage with the Holy Spirit.

KEY 1:

RELATIONSHIP

WIRED FOR RELATIONSHIP

We are wired for relationship with God, ourselves, and others. When asked by a Pharisee what the greatest commandment in the law was, "Jesus replied, 'Love the Lord your God with all your heart and with all your soul and with all your mind'" (Matthew 22:37, NIV). He proceeded to say "And the second is like it: 'Love your neighbor as yourself'" (Matthew 22:39, NIV). He concluded by saying something very dramatic and of great significance: "All the Law and the Prophets hang on these two commandments" (Matthew 22:40, NIV). It is quite remarkable that Jesus would say that. These words of Jesus are profound. He places our relationship with Him, and then with ourselves and others, above every law. He literally hinges the fulfillment of all law on these two commandments. He knew that our entire well-being and shalom stems from our relationship with Him, ourselves, and others. These commands of God are not mere rules and regulations. If the scales are removed from our eyes, we would start to see what this really means, how it applies to our daily lives, and what rest there is for us in these words of Jesus. What we can perceive as a religious command is actually something that is meant only for our well-being and success in all things.

God in His eternal wisdom did not command us to first love our neighbor or even our spouses or children. He did not command us to pray and fast and tithe and serve in church! As much as these are most definitely vital to a Christian life, Jesus clearly put the love relationship with God above all the other commands of God. We can impose a lot of expectations on ourselves and on those around us, but God knows and understands our weaknesses and our frailties. We can get entangled in all kinds of webs in our lives. We can even take pride in the busyness of life and all of the good activities in our efforts to be good people, good Christians, or to please God. But our souls do not find rest until we make our love relationship with God a priority.

As we make loving the Lord our God with all our heart, all our soul, and all our strength our first priority, and then loving ourselves and others as ourselves the second, all else falls in place.

We are then able to love ourselves, not lie or steal, to honor our parents, etc. and as we live life this way, God's blessings cannot help but invade our lives. We make life way harder than it is meant to be by focusing on our performances. And it is not really hard to love a God who loves us first, who takes away our sin, pain, shame, and blame, directs us, provides for us, and who becomes our loving Father and best friend. God reminds me repeatedly that the primary purpose and calling of my life, and everybody else's, is to focus on and nurture my relationship with Him and seek His Kingdom in all things. He promises that He is then able to add all these things that our hearts desire to our lives. Nothing else matters more than our relationship with Him.

As much as we are to revere God the Almighty and have the reverential fear of the Lord so we don't forget who He is, we are also invited to walk with Him, talk with Him, and develop our relationship with Him as Father and Friend. And this should be no surprise since the God who created the world with His command was also the One who walked with Adam in the cool of the day (Genesis 3:8). This invitation is endless because our God is without beginning or end. It is a lifelong journey to get to know Him more and more intimately until He becomes more real to us than the people around us. Ephesians 3:12, NIV, tells us that "in him (Jesus) and through faith in him we may approach God with freedom and confidence." We are to have a kind of relationship that is based on our faith in Jesus, and we are allowed unfettered access to God without anything holding us back. We are to feel fully free and confident in approaching Him.

WHAT DOES GOD EXPECT FROM US?

I am surrounded by amazing, gifted, and successful people who do not have a relationship with God. Why should they? They are educated, have good jobs, make good money, have good social lives, and are more or less happy people. Why should they believe in God? A God they do not see or hear. They see religious people around them. But they want to be free from religious shackles. They get their satisfaction from family and doing life the best they can. They are good people. I have been there. But I crossed the fence, and in following Christ and restoring my relationship with God, I have experienced the difference. The difference is in the state of the soul.

Is your soul rested and settled in knowing that today in life you are exactly where you are meant to be? Is there destiny and purpose in your life? How about if you were meant for greater things? The truth is that God does not call us to be religious people anyway. He is all about establishing a loving relationship. And if that's as far as you can get, that would be good enough for Him. He does not expect more from us. Anything more must stem from the place of overflow out of our relationship with Him. When we are immersed in His love and see ourselves as the Father sees us, it changes everything we know about ourselves. We experience love and life for the first time. We are set free and restored to be who we are created to be, and we are able to step into our individual highly creative lives. Once we get there, we are grafted in His plans and purposes for us and our spheres of influence. It must all arise from that place of restful relationship with Him though. And unless we have a relationship with God and learn to hear His voice and see Him at work in our lives, we can pursue paths that seem right to us and never really find true fulfillment, joy, and rest.

However, sometimes as Christians we can get shackled by the "God expectations" put on us. What does God expect from us? What do we have to do to be worthy followers of Christ? How much do we give? How much do we serve? How many missions do we get involved in? Can we sit in church week after week and never get involved in these things? How do we even give out of our debts? How do we serve out of our brokenness? How do we get involved in missions when we ourselves are drawing empty? How do we pray for others when our own sickness and pain is overwhelming us? I have learned that God expects our all and yet nothing from us until He has deposited in us what He is able to use to manifest His Kingdom. He does not expect anything out of a sense of duty or obligation. People and organizations can expect much from us, but God asks for one thing above all: love the Lord your God with all your heart (first), and love your neighbor next. Jesus tells us in Matthew 6:33 (ESV) to "Seek first the kingdom of God," which is "righteousness, peace and joy in the Holy Spirit" (Romans 14:17, NIV). When we pursue the "firsts" first, then God is able to usher in the next in our lives. We must focus on what's important.

The only worthwhile things that stand for eternity are the ones that are birthed out of this place of relationship and rest. In writing to the Corinthians, Paul tells them that "if anyone builds using gold, silver, costly stones, wood, hay or straw, their work will be shown for what it is" (1 Corinthians 3:12–13, NIV). It will be tested by fire. Clearly, not everything we do will stand the test of eternity. Why struggle and strive for results that may be meaningless and not even survive in the light of eternity?

STAGES OF REST

> As we walk with Him, He first gives us rest. Then as we grow in Him, He becomes our rest. And as we mature in Him, we become His resting place.

As a new Christian, He gives us a deep love for Him. As He gives us answers to life's questions and solutions to our problems, and we find Him true and faithful, we start to trust Him and the inner rest and peace in our lives grows. We have finally found someone who understands us completely, someone we can rely on, someone who will not let us down. The newfound relationship gives us much rest. Everyone's walk with God is different because He finds us all in our own unique places in life. But as immature Christians, many times we are first and foremost looking to God to help us out of the messy or painful situations He finds us in.

In my own life, I battled many insecurities. God came in and helped me restore my confidence. I saw the world with fresh eyes. I started to enjoy what was around me. There was a sense of being more alive than I had ever been. It took God a long time, or rather it took me a long time to partner with the Holy Spirit, to dig my way out of the emotional and mental holes I had sunk myself in. Then over time, I arrived at a place where I was looking to God as my rest. Situations in my life were not perfect. For example, the first few years of my married life were tumultuous, and I very quickly found myself on my knees developing my relationship with God until He became everything I needed. He satisfied me deep in my heart and emotions. I was not looking to people or circumstances in my life to sustain me. He became everything to me!

Today, I can boast a healthy marriage where me and my husband are best friends, yet God alone satisfies the deep needs in my heart and my life. Out of that place of rich abundance, I am able to build on a healthy marriage. Where there was once expectation, strife, anger over unmet expectations, and lack of understanding, today there is forbearance, longsuffering, patience, and love, the essential and key ingredients to any healthy relationship. Eventually, as we mature in our relationship with God and our communication with Him grows, we are able to be still in His presence, hear His voice, and follow the leading of His voice. As we do this, our lives start to line up with His plans for us, which are always good.

We are all invited to go further and continue to develop our relationship with Him until He is able to use us to minister to those around us, until He is able to start to impact our areas of influence and even the world through us. This is where we become His rest, a resting place where His presence can find habitation because we have become carriers of His presence and doers of His Word. We are invited to become His tabernacle, His temple.

> We can become so intimate with Him that we hear His heartbeat. When we talk, He listens, and when He talks, we hear Him. That is true rest.

And everybody is invited. How far do you want to go with Him? How deep do you want to go with Him? How intimate do you want to become with the Almighty God, your Papa, your Friend? He always has and continues to invite us to partner with Him.

HOW DO WE LOVE GOD FIRST?

How do we use this key to unlock restful living, when things are not working out, when the pressures of life build up, or when things seem to be falling apart? In the midst of trials, tribulations, and storms, remind yourself that you have one duty above all: to love the Lord your God with all your heart, strength, and mind. Literally take a moment or two or whatever it takes to focus in on your relationship with God. Learn to simply stop and restore this love relationship with the Creator. That is our first and foremost calling.

In His eternal wisdom, He asks us to just put it all aside, come to Him, let Him love on us, and love Him back when we are ready because in allowing Him to love us, He takes away our worries, fears, and anxieties and replaces them with love for

Him. Once we are able to love Him, we have already conquered our fears, anxious thoughts, and the things inside us that keep us from the place of a loving relationship. Do not strive to fix whatever is wrong in your life; rather, "strive" to enter into His rest (Hebrews 4:11, ESV). Do whatever it takes. Walk away from situations if you can. Take some time off. Get in your prayer closet. Do whatever it takes to get to that still place where you can focus on your relationship with God. Open your heart and spirit to allow Him to love on you. Love Him back, knowing He is the restorer of your soul.

In Him, you will find your rest, and not only rest but also everything else you need to tackle life from that place of rest. He gives freely. Rest to the weary, wisdom, strength.... The banquet is laid out; what do you need? He invites you to partake of Him.

For example, if someone is going through a difficult marriage, difficult relationships with children or at work to a point where there is constant pain and strife in the relationship, what does someone do? A Christian may seek prayer and Christian counseling. That is wonderful and can bear great results at reconciliation. What would happen though if one would choose to stop all striving and just choose to focus on God and deepen their relationship with Him? Choosing to take Him at His Word that He will take care of all things, that He will bring him/her out of this situation and restore love and peace, for that has to be the will of God.

How about if they choose to seek His Kingdom and come to a place of rest. Not because the situation is resolved but in spite of it. The soul might scream at us for a bit and push to action out of a place of anger, fear, insecurity, or turmoil. But if we would choose not to allow that to shake us but as an act of will allow the spirit to take over and overrule the fighting in the flesh and stay at a place where we can rest in the partnership and relationship with our loving God, we would still maintain our identities and be fruitful even in the season of turmoil. It would keep us from going in a downward, dark spiral as many do through difficulties and challenges of life. We can live at a place of hope, trusting in a good, just God to bring forth a good outcome. Not only that, but this would then allow us to see our situation from His perspective, and we may realize it is actually we who need to make a change or forgive or not allow past hurts to block change.

In today's culture, we can get so busy doing stuff that might appear to be beneficial that we can lose sight of what is really important. In my own life, every day I have to make choices. Do I run my kids from activity to activity? Do I volunteer at church every weekend? Do I offer to do more in my workplace to be helpful? Do I host a small group from church at my home every week? As fun, useful, nice and beneficial as each one of these is, if it brings me to a place of unrest and I lose sight of my relationship and rest with God, then I have to say no. Above all things, I choose to operate out of a place of rest where I am maintaining my relationship with God. Again and again, I find if I do that, all other things do fall in place. When chores are screaming at me to get done, if I am able to take time to hook up to Him, there is renewed energy, direction, and peace.

There are times when in moments of panic during the morning schedule as I realize I am late getting to work, I have given in to the pressure of the moment and hustled the kids, slammed doors, gotten myself in a huff, and left feeling drained. That is the kind of day I need my coffee as soon as I get to work, and I can't wait to get back home to reunite with my kids after the way I hustled and jostled them off in the morning. My focus in these moments is simply on what needs to be done next. Getting to work on time seems to take precedence over everything else and dictates how I think, feel, and what I do in that moment. What a waste! On other days, I have also in those moments reminded myself that I need to hold on to the restful place that God offers me. Doesn't He promise that if we seek His Kingdom, all else will be added unto us? Doesn't He, over everything, command us to love Him?

As I dig my heels in and remain in my restful place, I am flooded with love for my child who's not cooperating. I have a strategy for my next move. Not only that, but time seems to bow. I have never missed a school bus or been late to work when I have operated with God's Spirit in that situation. I get to work knowing God is with me. I am going to make a difference in the workplace today or in someone's life today. And if I don't, God is making a difference in my life. I urge you to try it for yourself.

It is amazing how the Creator of the universe gets deeply involved with our lives as we allow Him and make room for Him. Just by focusing on Him. Just by choosing to rest in His ability. It is not hard. It is the pathway to life. It is the pathway to creating what will stand in the light of eternity.

Your separation from your maker is a roadblock to the highly creative and satisfying life there is for you. Are you connected to the giver of life? If your answer is no, then surely how do you expect to experience the limitless life He offers? You then live and work and do all things with the finite potential inside of you—your mind, emotions, and intellect. You operate within your finite resources and feel limited. What do you look to for refueling? Recharging? reenergizing? In our modern-day world, there is so much out there that we can numb our minds and emotions until something gives and we are able to see ourselves for who we are and the missing pieces. I am convinced we miss out on the best by living that way. Allow yourselves to imagine a source of life within you that allows you to refuel as you have a need. No more running on reserve. Then know that this is available to all of us. Relationship is the first key to living a life of rest.

KEY 2:

IDENTITY

OUR PERCEPTION OF OUR IDENTITIES

We all perceive life to be a gift, a blessing, or something good that has been given to us. When the voices of our defeats and failures are tuned out and the scars and traumas of life are overlooked, we have the knowing in us that in some way we were created to be special and unique, and in that stillness we are able to experience the deep sense of destiny and purpose in us. Not only do most of us navigate life consciously and subconsciously, attempting to remain in realms that allow us to experience this, but life circumstances, people, and a voice within us never give up in attempting to direct us to that place. But unless we have a relationship with God and perceive His voice and His hand working in our lives, we can ignore this voice and direction, continue on paths that seem right to us, and never really find true fulfillment and joy in our lives.

A vast majority of us simply have no clue how to discover our destiny-ordained identities; we find ourselves helpless to get there and trapped in circumstances. Deep in us is the reality of who we really and truly are meant to be. Oftentimes when we look in the mirror, we don't recognize ourselves because life brings us so far from who we think we should be or what our lives should look like. No wonder most people see themselves as good people, even people who have committed crimes and no goodness is visible in their lives. They speak from who they were meant to be, and deep in them that identity continues to cling to them, even though in reality they have failed to realize it. Oftentimes, we take on identities and roles that don't even define us anymore. We get trapped in what we need to do to survive or fulfill responsibilities life places on us. I see more than one person who is tired and weary of the work they do for a living, their lifestyles, their finances, and just from the demands of life. They feel trapped by their circumstances and who they have become. And we tend to accept this as a part of life. And we can simply get swept along that path.

Often our identities are based on how people perceive us, what they say about us, or how they treat us. So much of what adults turn into can be a net result of how they got treated by people in life growing up. I frequently tell my children to remember that God created them special, they are gifted and talented, they are loved by God, His hand of protection is always over them, and that no matter what anyone says about them, they are what God says they are. I even tell them that if I am ever upset with them and say something that is not positive, then to use filters and not believe it but only believe what God says about them. My hope is to raise three children who are groomed to walk in their divine destinies. Even if they choose to walk away from it for a period, I am confident they will return to it (Proverbs 22:6).

In this media-driven world, we can derive our sense of identity from the stuff we post on media and the people who follow us. We would be lost if that was suddenly taken away from us. We must not be those who see ourselves as others see us, a product of generational hand-me-downs, the good and bad life hands out to us, our upbringing, and the roles we take on ourselves. We must not simply accept that we need jobs to make money, raise our families, and then get old and die with as many wonderful experiences as possible thrown in through the journey. We must know who we are from an eternal perspective. Unless we walk in our God-ordained identities, we cannot live restful lives.

HOW DOES GOD SEE US?

I have wonderful, lovely parents. And much of how I look and conduct my life comes from them. But I am also a child of God. My deeper identity as a human being, my deeper knowing of myself, and deeper wisdom to live life from an eternal perspective comes from Him. I know who I am because I know who my God is. And in that knowledge and revelation, I have deep rest. We are lost until we establish a relationship with our Creator. We start to discover our true identities once we see ourselves as God sees us. Only in His light do we find out who He has called us to be.

God invites us all to say goodbye to the hurts and pains of our pasts, the generational influences that might be holding us captive, and the ills that others or our circumstances might have inflicted on us. He invites us to a clean slate where He can then rewrite our lives. It is never too late for Him. He has all the tools necessary to bring us back to our original design and then help us rise to become everything He has called each one of us to be. To Him, it doesn't matter where you've been in life or how far you've drifted from being His original intent for you. He is able to use all of that in ridiculously unbelievable ways to use it for your benefit. It is true, friends, that "in all things God works for the good of those who love him" (Romans 8:28, NIV). Once we choose to align ourselves with His calling for us, He is able to take all of the negative baggage from us, replace it with His own glorious nature, and transform us into our original blueprint. We must participate in the process and allow Him to do what only He can do.

RISING TO OUR TRUE IDENTITIES

We know God created mankind in His own image and likeness (Genesis 1:27). God extends His Glory through us. After all, how can the unlimited One contain it all without giving it away? It is His nature to give. Without measure. Pressed down, without limits. He is the giver of all good things. His very own limitless life is extended to us, the highest of His creation. God's desire is to extend His glory through us. We were always meant to be carriers of God's glory. Adam forfeited His identity. His God image and God calling were marred by embracing sin. Since then, God has done everything with the intention to curb sin and restore man's identity. Before the coming of Jesus, the law was given to keep sin in check. In sending Jesus, the sin factor was dealt with once and for all. We are all invited to follow Jesus. In doing so, our old man with its sin-tarnished nature is crucified, and we are given a new life in Christ.

We are told in 2 Corinthians 5:17, NIV, that "if anyone is in Christ, the new creation has come: The old is gone, the new is here!" Our identities are restored to us, as children of God, created in His own image and likeness. The Bible tells us in 1 John 4:17, ASV, that "as he is, even so, are we in this world." We must not look at ourselves, our flesh, and our circumstances. We must start to appropriate God's Word by faith. We must believe and confess God's Word over ourselves. This is to be our identity.

We are to live as Christ lived in this world. Yes, we are still in this broken, sinful world, and yes, we will make mistakes. But God has made provision for it. The blood of Jesus is all powerful to wipe away our sin and put it away as far as the east is from the west. We are not to grovel in our sin or remorse over it, but receive the forgiveness of Christ to wipe away the baggage of shame, blame, and pain that is easy for us to pick up. We must accept who God says we are. Romans 3:22, NIV, clearly tells us that "righteousness is given through faith in Jesus Christ to all who believe." 2 Corinthians 5:21, NIV, tells us that "God made him who had no sin to be sin for us, so that in him we might become the righteousness of God." This righteousness is a gift (Romans 5:15). A huge price was paid in order that we could be made righteousness, just like the first man, who was created sinless in order that God's original intention for man and for the world might be fulfilled.

What if all Christians truly start to believe and receive our identities as God sees us? Who does God say we are? He pronounces us righteous; He pronounces us blameless. The Bible tells us that just as He is, also are we in this world (1 John 4:17). No more are we pitiful humans ravaged by the sin factor, sad, depressed, nervous, afraid, unhealthy, and somehow at the mercy of God who sometimes gives us health and sometimes sends sickness our way to teach us lessons. God tells us we are righteous, we are holy. If we are His body and He is our Head, how can we be sick, unhealthy, or sinful?

We must rise to our full identities. We must believe the Word of God, cooperate with the Holy Spirit, and rise up to become everything we are called to be. Romans 8:19, NIV, tells us that "creation waits in eager expectation for the children of God to be revealed." We must rise up to be those who receive what God has to offer to us so we can fulfill His original plan. We must accept that we are sinless and blameless in His eyes and pleasing to Him. We must accept the authority and dominion over creation that He has always offered us. We cannot do this until we accept our identities as God sees us. We must allow the Holy Spirit to bring us into His freedom and glory so we can fulfill His purpose, so His Kingdom may come here on earth, and His will be done on earth as in Heaven. Romans 8:21,

NIV, states "creation itself will be liberated from its bondage to decay and brought into the freedom and glory of the children of God." He wants us to know who we are. He wants us to understand the potential He has put inside each one of us. He wants us to rule and reign.

Creation is waiting for the sons and daughters of the Almighty Creator to break off the shackles of false identity, to take ownership of who He has created us to be, to embrace our destinies, to take back what has been lost, and restore to the world the original intent of God. That is why we pray, Your Kingdom come, Your will be done on earth as it is in Heaven.

HOW DO WE FIND OUR IDENTITIES?

We are all called to be sons and daughters of God, but we are all not the same. We all have our individual blueprint that no one else has. As sons and daughters of God and in the light of our relationship with God, we discover our gifts and talents, our creativity, and our calling. We must drown out other voices. We must not believe our flesh, the voices of other people, or the circumstances in our lives to tell us who we are. We must only believe who God says we are. If the Spirit within us justifies us, then let us not listen to the voice of blame.

If God says we are able, then let us not highlight the weaknesses of our flesh; instead, let's declare what God says over us. If the Spirit is pointing us to a path that our logic and reasoning does not fully comprehend, let's take the path, let's not be afraid. Let's say no to the lure of anything that does not appear to be from God. Let's be diligent to not get sidetracked but stay on the path of our divinely ordained destinies. Let us hitch our creativity to the Creator's. Let's engage with our gardens and tend and take care of them. Let's rise up to become who each one of us is called to be and influence the realms we are called to influence. Let's become the glorious bride of Christ, His body, the ones who match the glory of the Head.

We cannot do any of this in our finite strength. We must allow and partner with the Holy Spirit. Allow me to take you through the story in Luke 8:22–25, when Jesus gets in a boat with His disciples and has them go with Him to the other side of the shore. The story goes on to tell us that Jesus falls asleep in the boat. I believe it was a purposeful sleep because He was about to teach His disciples an important lesson. A storm comes and the boat starts to fill with water. In the natural, it did not look good. Imagine the scenario: a sailboat filled with people, winds raging, and water starting to fill it up. It obviously drove fear into the hearts of His disciples, and they woke Him up. I wonder what kinds of thoughts went through their heads before they decided to wake Him up. Were they upset with Him, did they wonder how He could sleep while they were in danger, did they secretly blame Him in their hearts for not caring? The story ends well because Jesus wakes up, commands the winds and waves to stop. It all ceased, and calm was restored. Jesus rebuked His disciples for their lack of faith.

We have all heard this story and learned lessons in faith and trusting God. But let's go beyond that and throw the spotlight on Jesus. First, I believe that this sleep was intentional because He was about to teach an important lesson to His disciples. Second, I believe with all my heart that Jesus could sleep that way because He knew who He was. He knew God had a plan for His life, and nothing could change that. And in knowing His identity, He knew the authority He carried as the Son of God, that winds and waves were no match for what He carried in Him, the very anointed presence of His Father.

The Bible tells us in 1 John 4:17, NIV, that "In this world, we are like Jesus." We are to "live like Jesus here in this world" (NLT). How is that possible? Our flesh will tell us we cannot. But our spirit leaps up in us and tells us that is true. And we are "not in the realm of the flesh but are in the realm of the Spirit, if indeed the Spirit of God lives in you" (Romans 8:9, NIV). So, while we are in this world we are like Jesus—clearly not in our flesh but in our spirit. And as long as we allow ourselves to be led by the Spirit of God, we can have the very life and rest Jesus had. The Spirit of God Himself will teach us how we can be like Jesus. How can we sleep or in essence be in such a place of rest that even when life-threatening storms are brewing around us, we can be at complete rest?

In doing so, the trajectory of our lives shifts to a God-ordained one. As we are set free from the fear and insecurity that can hold us captive, we are freed to take risks and follow Jesus as He calls us to walk on water with Him. We don't need to see the results of our decisions anymore. As long as we hear the Shepherd and follow His voice, our decisions will draw us closer to where we need to go.

> We cannot be at rest until we are set on the path to become who we are called to be, sons and daughters of the most-high God.

KEY 3:

RIGHT BELIEVING/FAITH

FAITH VERSUS DEFIANCE

When Adam was given the command to eat from any tree in the Garden of Eden but not from the tree of knowledge of good and evil or else he "would certainly die" (Genesis 2:17, NIV), it required both Adam and Eve's trust in God and in His Word. They had to believe that God was in no way withholding something good from them that they needed to have. They had to believe in His goodness. They had to believe that God really meant this for their good. They needed to have faith in God, His plan, and provision. What happened when Eve was presented with the lure of eating fruit that would cause her "eyes will be opened," and she would "be like God, knowing good and evil"? (Genesis 3:5, NIV). She now saw the fruit as something that not only looked "good for food and pleasing to the eye" but was also "desirable for gaining wisdom" (Genesis 3:6, NIV).

Eve was deceived. She was now able to justify to herself why it was okay to defy the boundaries God laid out for them. After all, the fruit looked good, and then there was the wisdom to be had in knowing more of good and evil. She inadvertently believed the lie that God perhaps did not want them to be like Him and know what He knew. The Bible does not give us details, but I imagine she talked with Adam about it and they both agreed it was okay to check it out. Due to their lack of faith in God's goodness and resulting disobedience, mankind lost his restful land, a land of delight and pleasure. The seeds of unbelief had been sown into humanity.

God has continued to steer humanity out of unbelief and sin to see Him for who He is, a good God, who created man in His image to inhabit this world, have dominion, and inherit God's blessing. He has done everything to pave the way for us to return to the blessing. God's effort has always been to find those whose hearts belonged to Him, those who could see God for who He is, so they could reclaim God's blessing, reclaim their identity, and reclaim their dominion. Let's fast forward through history as we see what God was weaving through generations.

These included Noah and the great flood, which wiped out sinful humanity at that time. At the tower of Babel, people were scattered to annihilate their pride and rebellion. Abraham was a man who found great favor with God and was promised descendants, the promised land, and blessings. He received

His promised son, Isaac, who became the father of Jacob, later renamed Israel. Jacob's son Joseph became the king of Egypt and was succeeded by generations of Israelites in Egypt.

After he died, the new king turned the Israelites into slaves. Israel were God's chosen people in whom God demonstrated His Kingdom until the coming of the redeemer, the seed, the One who would then reconcile all to God. God rescued the Israelites from years of bondage to the Egyptians with great might and power and gave them many promises with many demonstrations of miracles. However, we see that despite all of the demonstrations of God's power toward the Israelites with the difficulties they encountered, they forgot God's promises and failed to trust Him. They took matters into their own hands, went completely astray, and even created their own gods and allowed sin to enter into their lives. The Israelites who perished on the way and never made it to their promised land did so from lack of faith and resulting disobedience.

GOD WAITS ON US

God still waits on us. Waits for us to see Him for who He is so we can become who we are created to be and reclaim the blessing and dominion offered to us. Just like the Israelites, God brings each one of us out of the places He finds us in, with demonstrations of His love for us and His power in our lives. He gives us many promises through His Word and inscribed in our hearts. Today we have the same challenge. We are given all of God's promises in the Bible. God also gives each one of us promises for our lives. Will we be those who believe until we see the fruition of these promises? Are we those who can rest in the assurance of His promises and not feel that somehow we will get shortchanged if we don't take matters into our own hands? We do not want to be like Adam who could not believe that God laid some boundaries for his good, crossed the line, and in turn lost everything God had for him. We do not want to be like the Israelites who, despite seeing God's hand at work so powerfully in their lives, could not hold on to their faith when things did not appear to be quite what they wanted to see and did not make it to their promised land.

> Surely, in order to inherit our restful land, our Edens, we must believe in God and His unshakeable goodness toward us. He is not only able but passionately desires to fulfill His promises in our lives.

HOW DOES FAITH OPERATE?

We all walk paths in our lives where we don't see clearly what God is doing. If we look at our situation, it might seem as if we cannot rest in our faith alone. We feel like we will somehow miss something if we don't take matters in our own hands and do something about it. We are so attuned to the world culture that we start to live in a paradigm where it is all up to us. We leave no room for God in our lives. But "without faith it is impossible to please God, because anyone who comes to him must believe that he exists and that he rewards those who earnestly seek him" (Hebrews 11:6, NIV). Why must we believe? It is simple.

> Our faith brings us away from the clamor in our heads, the confusion in our lives, the actions that stem from trying to find solutions to the difficulties we face. Our faith causes us to be still in front of Him. It brings us to the place of rest. In our faith lies a key that brings us to rest.

And once the clamor in our worlds comes to a place of stillness, we start to see Him. We start to hear what He is saying to us. Oftentimes, if we are still enough, we start to see what He is doing in our situation. God always is. He is always for us. He is always strong on our behalf. Psalm 37:7, NIV urges us to "Be still before the Lord and wait patiently for him." The Passion Translation of the Bible paraphrases this verse beautifully "quiet your heart in his presence and pray; keep hope alive as you long for God to come through for you." His spirit is always available to show us the way out of our difficulties. Our lack of faith, however, causes us to go into an uproar, and it becomes difficult for us to hear His voice, see what He wants us to do, or which way He wants us to go. That is when we start to question God and His goodness. We start to pray desperate, pleading prayers, not being able to see that God is on our side, has the answers to all our problems, and is passionate about helping us out of each one of them (Psalm 34:19).

Our lack of faith causes our experience to become one
arising from our difficulty versus from His solution.

There are numerous stories in the Bible that show us how faith operates in the lives of those who believed in Him in the midst of their adversities. In Daniel chapter 6, we see that Daniel was trapped in a decree orchestrated by jealous administrators and satraps of King Darius's kingdom because they did not want him to be made administrator over the entire kingdom. Despite King Darius's favor for Daniel and recognition of his excellent work, he was forced to follow through with his decree and have Daniel thrown into a lion's den with hungry lions. To everyone's surprise and wonder, Daniel spent the night in the lion's den and emerged unscathed the next morning. According to Daniel "My God sent his angel, and he shut the mouths of the lions. They have not hurt me, because I was found innocent in his sight" (Daniel 6:22, NIV).

In another story in Daniel chapter 3, we see the popular story of Shadrach, Mishak, and Abednego who were thrown into a blazing furnace for refusing to bow to the gold statue of King Nebuchadnezzar. The king was so enraged by their refusal to bow to the statues or worship his gods that he ordered the furnace to be heated seven times hotter than usual. The fire was so hot that the soldiers who were ordered to throw the three men into the fire were all killed by the flames. But what happened to these three men was truly amazing. In fact, the narration tells us that King Nebuchadnezzar was so awed that he "leaped" up (Daniel 3:24, NIV) in amazement: "Look! I see four men walking around in the fire, unbound and unharmed, and the fourth looks like a son of the gods" (Daniel 3:25, NIV). He commanded them to come out, and he and his officials crowded around them. "They saw that the fire had not harmed their bodies, nor was a hair of their heads singed; their robes were not scorched, and there was no smell of fire on them" (Daniel 3:27, NIV). What a testimony to the faith of these men!

HOW DO WE BELIEVE WHEN WE DON'T SEE?

What does it mean to live by faith? Google defines faith as a "complete trust or confidence in someone or something."[1] Let's look at the Hebrew root of the word *faith*. The Hebrew word for faith is *Emunah*, which literally means "something or someone that is firm in their actions." The root word of *Emunah* is *Aman*, which means "firm or something that is supported or secure." God is certainly firm in His actions. Not just His Word.

Clearly, in both of these stories, the people who are targeted are faced with some pretty severe challenges. The lions and the fiery furnace were both very real. They stood face-to-face, even enveloped by extremely fearsome situations. But these men chose not to allow themselves to be swept by fear but rather stand in faith, trusting the Almighty God. How could they do that? Simply because they knew Him! They knew their God. They knew His power. They believed He was their protector and Savior. And even if He did not come through for them situationally, they knew Him enough to know they would always worship Him because He was the One true Almighty God.

The result of their faith was amazing. They continued to be respectful to the king but did not hesitate to let him know they were unwilling to worship him or his so-called gods. No fear was seen in Daniel as he was thrown into the lion's den, and he emerged unscathed. No fear or resistance was seen in the three men Shadrach, Mishak, and Abednego as they were thrown into the fiery furnace. The guards who threw them into the furnace were instantly killed, but these three men emerged without a single hair on their head singed and not even the smell of fire on them. These men knew and trusted their God. Can we walk through difficult situations in our lives with such complete trust in the Lord that there is no smell of fire or smoke on us, or do we make it to the finish line harassed, upset, and complaining? God's plan for us is way more than us merely getting by in this life.

Here is something I have learned in life: we *will* face difficulties. The Bible is clear about it. Talking to His disciples, Jesus tells them "in this world you will have trouble" (John 16:33, NIV). His Word applies to each one of us. It is unlikely that you and I will ever be thrown into a lion's den or a fiery furnace, but we all have our challenges we get to face. We all get to stand face-to-face with difficulties that scare us. We might find ourselves in the midst of a fiery situation with no way to escape. How do we feel when we are in the midst of unfair situations? When things are said to us that are unjust? When people don't understand us? When we suffer consequences of other people's actions, even those who are close to us such as our friends, spouses, or children?

I have had moments in my life where I had to confront lions. I have had long seasons in which I felt as if I was in a fiery furnace. With no way to escape. I had to make a choice. Is God who He says He is? Is He really a good God? Does He really care about me? Is He able to deliver me from the difficult situations in my life? How do we keep our faith in a God we don't see, sometimes don't hear? What if He doesn't come through? Am I not supposed to do all I can to defend myself, protect myself, and take control over situations? Do I sit around doing nothing? Do I allow myself to be thrown to the lion's den and into the fiery furnaces of life? In Isaiah 30:15 (ESV) when faced by an Assyrian attack, Israel and Judah turned to Egypt for help instead of turning to God.

They trusted in Pharaoh's strength rather than God's counsel and wisdom. They were a people who had been set apart to be God's people in whom God would be manifest. Instead of faith in the Almighty God, in their moment of crisis, they chose to put their trust in the strength of Egypt. Then the Word of the Lord came to them, "In returning and rest you shall be saved; in quietness and in trust shall be your strength." How often do we do that as Christians? When faced with difficulties and challenges, do we run to things that might look like they can provide us with a solution? Or do we put our trust in the Lord who is not only able but always willing to help us? We must rest in Him. And He will surely point us the way, deliver us, give us wisdom, provide us with a way out, and even do a miracle for us. Can we continue to have faith when the answer is slow to come? Does that mean God is not going to help us? Certainly not.

In our quietness, His Word prevails; in our trust, His trustworthiness prevails; and in our rest, His action prevails.

FAITH AND REST

Without faith, the responses of our flesh typically are fear, worry, anxiety, confusion, acting quickly, retaliating, defending ourselves, fighting back, etc. How about if we were to choose to remain at rest irrespective of what is going on within or around us and act/speak once the way of peace is clear to us, until God shows us what to do, which way to go? Rest then becomes the place that connects us to this faith, and our faith keeps us in this place until we can confidently say, "the Lord will perfect that which concerns me" (Psalm 138:8, NKJV).

If we believe that God is who He says He is, if we believe in His goodness toward us, if we believe his Word to be true, and that all of His promises are yes and amen to us in Christ Jesus (2 Corinthians 1:20), then rest is the place where we appropriate these promises, and our faith brings us there. Believe, believe, believe. Replace every negative thought with what God thinks, and replace every negative word with what God says. Believe until you come to rest.

That is all God asks us to do. In John 6:28–30, NIV, Jesus's disciples ask Him, "What must we do to do the works God requires?" "Jesus answered, 'The work of God is this: to believe in the one he has sent.'" That can be a little difficult to wrap our minds around in a culture where it's all about doing, where even our Christian lives are about doing, serving, giving, praying, reading, fellowshipping, and going to church. All of these are absolutely necessary for us to walk our Christian walk fully. However, they cannot replace the state of our hearts. And with God, He is more concerned about our hearts than anything else. Can we believe Him? Can we take Him at His Word? Can our faith in Him bring us to a restful place in Him? Jesus says to us "Come to me, all of you who are weary and carry heavy burdens, and I will give you rest. Take my yoke upon you. Let me teach you, because I am humble and gentle at heart, and you will find rest for your souls. For my yoke is easy to bear, and the burden I give you is light" (Matthew 11:28–30, NLT).

KEY 4:

FREEDOM

THE STATE OF OUR HEADS AND HEARTS

There is rest in being free. I believe in our hearts we all want to be free and limitless, yet we don't know how. We find ourselves limited by our personalities, fears, anxieties, by how other people see us, by our life experiences, and so much more. We are bound by habits, thought patterns, forces of darkness, or just plain ignorance. We can become slaves to a myriad of things because they start to dictate how we live our lives. This could be our work, the pursuit of money, people, habits, temptations, etc. If we were to examine our hearts at any given moment, we would be surprised by how many things are bothering us or causing us anxiety and how driven we are by what's going on in our heads and hearts. I am not sure we fully comprehend all the stuff that ties us up in knots on the inside, threatening to take us captive to its engulfing tentacles.

Interpersonal relationships could be a huge source of negative feelings that drown out our inner freedom. Day-to-day conflicts, unmet expectations, fear of not meeting expectations of others, being offended by others, and our inability to forgive others can hold us captive for all of our lives. Our perceptions, discontentment with ourselves, the inability to love ourselves, and be at peace can constantly limit us. Being fearful and anxious about situations, people, and our future is perhaps an overriding theme in our heads, even when we are not aware of it. These then start to dictate how we live, the decisions we make, and we walk tied and bound by these things. How many of us can say we are truly free in our hearts today?

I remember being there in life, tossed by every wind, even as a faith-filled Christian. Maybe we even consider this a normal way to live. We engage in different coping mechanisms to deal with these things as we struggle to find some release from these knots that threaten to choke the life out of us. We might drown it all with busyness and entertainment. After all, an hour spent on Facebook posting some wonderful pictures and looking at all the other wonderful stuff people post can make us feel so much better. With conflict in interpersonal relationships, we might give in to gossip, put others down, or harden our hearts to escape from the emotional turmoil that comes from it. We might, in turn, lose relationships or distance ourselves from people. At work, we might overwork to be noticed or underwork to get some rest. We might switch jobs but may never be truly content because we can't find that perfect job. Worse still is when we walk away from our marriages leaving a tangle of unresolved stuff that threatens to dictate the rest of our lives. We are bound and tied down daily, no matter where we are, and there are those knots in our stomachs, hearts, or heads we can't get rid of.

Can we really be free from these? Are we not supposed to just deal with these? If it gets too bad, we can use counseling services, and if our minds give out under the weight of distressing situations, well then, there are psychiatrists and medications to help. These therapies can be good, and I am sure they have helped countless people. Yet at the same time, do we get bound to something else? And do we find the freedom we seek? We can consider this to be just a normal part of life.

> It may be hard to believe that there is true freedom available to us until we see ourselves and our lives in the light of God and how He sees us and our circumstances.

WHAT DOES THE BIBLE SAY ABOUT FREEDOM?

It is clear that every person is born with a free will. We just have to take one look at our children to know that. Most parent–child conflict arises from the child's push to exercise his/her will and the parent's desire to control. We know that unless we find a happy medium, neither will be happy. After all, children are created with their inborn giftings. Childhood is their time to discover and pursue these. Our job is to nurture them in the direction of their gifting so they can become the people they are meant to be, and in doing that, influence the world as each one of us is called to.

To understand the true freedom offered to us by God, we have to return to history. Let us take a look at what kind of freedom was offered to the first man, Adam, and Eve. What God wanted for mankind then, He still wants today. God placed them in the beautiful, perfect creation He created to rule and reign over it. They had no enemies. They had all provision. They were offered each other's companionship, and God Himself walked and talked with them. They were offered incredible beauty and freedom. In fact, they were not created to comprehend anything other than that. I believe the tree of knowledge of good and evil was planted within their reach along with a clear communication of consequences of partaking from it, in order to ensure mankind's total freedom to choose. In the Garden of Eden, the tree of knowledge of good and evil was accessible to Adam, but he was warned that if he ate from that tree, he would surely die (Genesis 3:3, NKJV).

Adam and Eve chose the way of defiance, and sin and death were the result. By embracing something mankind was not wired for, they found themselves in bondage to fear, blame, shame, and pain almost immediately. His relationship with God was changed! Now he feared Him and hid from Him. Now mankind knew what sin was, and he had to constantly choose between right and wrong. Humanity, created in God's image, was wired for goodness and love. We were created to express God in this magnificent world. We were created to have indescribable freedom. But this had been lost. Our freedom lay in the choosing of life versus death.

Mankind's freedom lay in maintaining His relationship with God, not in hiding from Him.

Through the rise and fall and scattering of generations, there is the overriding theme of God attempting to restore freedom to a group of people who were His chosen people to exhibit His glory and power. We see this in His leading the Israelites out from their bondage to the Egyptians with the promise of a free land. God chose Moses to lead the Israelites out of their bondage to the Egyptians and into the promised land with giving them the Ten Commandments and the Mosaic Law to once again keep them on the path of life versus death and maintain their relationship with God. These guidelines were not meant to be mere restrictions on the freedom of people but in fact guidelines to keep humanity on a path of God's favor and blessings for their well-being and prosperity in all things.

With sin having seeped deep into the fabric of mankind and their lives, however, they struggled hopelessly. Even the law became a bone of contention and a tool to bind people down with its tenets. Jesus Himself was repeatedly chastised by the religious people who ultimately became the cause of His death on the cross. But we know as cruel as His death was, He was a willing partaker of it in order that His death would set us free from every sin, every bondage. He died to set the prisoner free. Human freedom is inextricably woven into our choosing of life and relationship with God. When freedom is used to choose what doesn't produce life, the result ultimately irrefutably leads us into bondage and ultimate loss of freedom.

Our freedom to choose is a gift that was hardwired into us by God who created us in His image, but we were never meant to use it to choose darkness and death. When we choose darkness, we become prisoners walking this life with chains and knots inside us that we are not hardwired to bear. We may look fine from the outside, but only we know the bondage we carry within us. We have a choice offered to us daily. Will we accept the freedom God offers us? The acceptance of this has practical implications that go deep and influence every aspect of our lives. True freedom is freedom from all the things that separate us from God.

FREEDOM IN OUR DAY-TO-DAY LIVES

In our day-to-day practical lives, in everything we think, speak, and do, we choose life and freedom or bondage and death. True freedom is indeed being free from sin. Hebrews 12:1, NIV, talks about sin as something "that so easily entangles." Also, Romans 6:23, NIV, says that "the wages of sin is death, but the gift of God is eternal life in Christ Jesus our Lord." We normally think of sin as something really bad and socially unacceptable. Killing someone and robbery certainly sound like sin, but Jesus was very clear that sin was also in the stuff that's inside of us— angry thoughts and judging others. Now, who doesn't do this?

Here's the thing though; these things are what steal our inner freedom in our daily lives. We are left with knots in our heads, hearts, and stomachs. These choke out our experience of life, and we instead embrace death—death of joy, death of peace, death of love—and in an expanding circle, these start to affect the decisions we make, and sometimes we invite sickness into our bodies via these negative spirals we sink into.

In embracing the cross, we embrace the death and destruction of all things negative. We are all invited to embrace a different trajectory in our journeys. We are invited to embrace self-acceptance, seeing and accepting others as God sees them, and we are able to slash these demons of negativity out of our lives as they appear and wipe them out of our minds, hearts, and lives. For example, let's say someone is mean to me, and I am hurt, offended, upset, and angry. I am truly facing an unfair situation. So, do I adjudicate my right to be upset, angry, and take vengeance? If I choose not to, then I seem to get entangled in a web with no release.

At the root of it is my own inability to be secure in who I am, my inability to not be offended, to see others as God sees them, to forgive as He forgives us, and in fact even respond in love. This is in defiance of God's command, which urges us to love others as we love ourselves. If we had this immense love for God, ourselves, and others, we would walk free of all such trauma. At the root of all bondage is a defiance of God's commands, which really keep us connected to Him and keep us walking in freedom. When we don't accept this invitation, we inadvertently open our hearts to negative spirits that take away our inner freedom and joy.

When I refer to freedom, I mean complete freedom on the inside—freedom in our hearts, our heads, and our emotions. Freedom to live and love. To love the Lord our God with all of our hearts, freedom to love our neighbor and ourselves. And freedom on the outside to be totally us, to pursue skills, jobs, and activities that engage our unique gifts and talents and live a life that satisfies us. And if we are not there, God invites us to partner with Him to slash all those obstacles that hinder us from living in this totally amazing gift of freedom He offers us.

> True freedom is when we are so free on the inside that we are able to walk in love no matter what.

THE INVITATION TO FREEDOM

Often people do not want God in their lives because they want to be free. But the paradox is that it is impossible to find true freedom until we find God and until we see Him for who He really is and ourselves as He sees us. We want to be free and limitless, yet we can refuse to connect with the Spirit of God and choose to remain limited and finite in our human potential. When we see God for who He is and our hearts open to Him, we are ready to embrace a different reality, a reality where we find true freedom. When we restore our relationship with our Creator, His spirit sets us free. 2 Corinthian 3:17, NIV, tells us that "the Lord is the Spirit, and where the Spirit of the Lord is, there is freedom."

We may see saying yes to God as a call to be subversive to God. Can the Creator and provider of all things require us to be slavish and do as He tells us to, foregoing the pleasures of this world? We are just not hardwired to want to believe in or follow a God who might perhaps ask for our life to go in a certain way or impose restrictions on the way we want to live. Rightfully so, we are created with a free will. We are created for freedom. To be. To live. To choose. So, what happens when we choose to accept the sacrifice paid for us on the cross by Jesus and choose to follow Him? Do we lose our freedom to live life the way we want to? Yes, we do lose our choice to live in a manner where we are clueless about where we are heading. We lose our choice to live without any awareness of our divine destiny and purpose. We lose our freedom to live with sin and its consequences. We get grafted into God's plan and purpose for our lives.

In finding our Maker, we gain a life where we finally choose to find ourselves in light of the One who created us. We find our gifts and callings, we find a life filled with love, joy, and peace, and we find rest. And once we do, there is no stopping us. Only Heaven truly becomes our limit.

ALLOWING GOD'S SPIRIT TO INVADE

Many people are clueless about where they are heading. Each day propels us, and we go from jobs to vacations, raising our kids, and we are still clueless. Once you say yes to God and accept the new life He offers, you must cooperate with His spirit, which then awakens in us, and allow Him to take charge so He can do with your life only what He can, in supernatural ways. Here's what I like my typical experience to be when bad stuff comes my way: I remind myself that my Father, and I know who He created me to be. I know my Father, His love for me, and His approval for who I am, even when I make mistakes. I know my Father and His plans for me. I know beyond a shadow of a doubt that He is for me. Yes, I have to correct myself as He shows me. Sometimes I have to ask for forgiveness. But He places such love in my heart for the sinner, the person who wrongs me. I see them as He sees them—vulnerable, yet created in the image of God, worthy but lost in sin and ignorance. He gives me forgiveness in my heart.

I have learned that offense is a bad spirit that can take me downhill so quickly that I do not want to invite it into my life. I am set free and happy because God has set me free from bondage to sin. I am not offended, I am not made upset by circumstances, and I am not worried about the future. No one can give me a bad deal because God always gives me a good deal out of all the bad that has been sown into my life by others. I am joyful. I see what God is doing in the midst of bad situations. I see people for who they would be if they knew

God as their loving Father. I do not fear my future because I know beyond a shadow of a doubt that "my redeemer lives" (Job 19:25, NIV), the One who vindicates me, the One who justifies me, the One who holds my future. If I can react this way, I am truly free!

We are all subject to something, or multiple things, through our lives until Jesus becomes the Lord of our lives. Without God, we are often people who are hurrying and scurrying, making it through life without clear direction, without roots, filled with temporal plans, and many filled with a sense of hopelessness, depression, anxiety and living without love or joy. We are bothered by so many things on a daily basis, by ourselves, by people around us, by situations. We can live much of our lives led by our fears, insecurities, and anxieties. We can make decisions based on past experiences. In all these, we are bound. There is rest in freedom, and freedom brings us to rest. We must look to Him. He has the keys to set us free into our highly creative lives. Once we get there, we are automatically grafted into His plans and purposes for the world. And we play our part. It must all arise from that place of restful relationship with Him though.

When the Bible asks us to lay ourselves down and carry the cross daily, it a charge to finally experience true freedom.

We are set on a path to experience freedom from pain, shame, and blame. Freedom from the pitiful ways in which we struggle and fumble through our lives, never quite arriving. Freedom from having to worry, be anxious, stressed, and falling short one way or the other. Freedom from striving and arriving at a place of rest. A place where peace, joy, and rest are the baseline. And everything that is of any significance comes only in abiding in that place.

What a wonderful invitation. But we must play our part in letting go and allowing the Spirit of truth to guide us. In a way, we are relinquishing all control for a life where we can focus on rising in our creative potentials and finally have the satisfaction of becoming who we were always meant to be, and as we grow in it, to have spheres of influence to impact the world with our gifts.

KEY 5:

PRESENCE

SHKHINAH GLORY

God's presence is not an ethereal concept. It is tangible. It can be discerned. It is weighty and palpable. His presence carries His glory. The literal meaning of glory derives from the Hebrew word *kavod*, also meaning "honor" and is linked to the word *kaved*, meaning "heavy."[1] I believe this is in the sense of what it carries, the very essence and element of God. And those of us who have experienced this glorious presence can testify that this presence causes us to bow. It is physically heavy from what it carries, besides causing us to bow in reverential honor of the God Almighty. Another word that is used in Jewish literature for glory is *Shkhinah*, the root word for *mishkan*, which is a word used for the tabernacle that Moses built signifying a "dwelling."² The word *Shkhinah* is used for the felt presence and visible manifestation of God's presence.

The earliest mention of God's presence in the Bible is in the story of creation. The story of creation in Genesis carries the picture of God's intention and vision for creating this world and mankind. Placing Adam and Eve in the Garden of Eden is the blueprint for how He wanted us to live our lives. We are told in Genesis 3:8, NKJV, speaking about Adam and Eve: "And they heard the sound of the Lord God walking in the garden in the cool of the day, and Adam and his wife hid themselves from the presence of the Lord God among the trees of the garden." This indeed reveals to us that it was God's intention that His experiential presence would be a part of mankind's life and that He would walk with us and talk with us.

Adam and Eve lost this privilege once they embraced sin and were banished from the Garden. But God's intention regarding creation and mankind remains unchanged, and since then God's heart has always been to manifest His presence to those whose hearts were right toward Him. We see this weaved through the stories of Abraham, Moses, Joshua, Noah, and all the way through the Old-Testament prophets. God has always been on the lookout to find Himself a few who would be after His heart, after His original plan for mankind. These are the ones He revealed His presence to. The biggest, most heart-wrenching laments in those generations have been from those who had tasted the presence of God and then lost it due to their disobedience in following God's plans and instead embracing sin.

The presence of God departing from Jerusalem resulted in the book of Lamentations being written with vivid renditions of the destruction of Jerusalem. In Psalm 51:11, David's heart cry is that God would not remove His Spirit from him. He knew he had sinned, and he had first-hand experience of what happened to Saul when he was forsaken by God because of His disobedience in not participating in God's plan after having been a man after God's heart. Not only did Saul commit unspeakable atrocities, but he himself was harassed by a tormenting spirit and lost his ability to even speak. In losing God's presence, these men seemed to lose the thing that was the most important to them.

GOD'S PRESENCE IS AVAILABLE TO US

Generations later, the never-changing God who is ever compassionate, long-suffering, and patient is still waiting on humankind to make the choice to return to His original intention for humanity. He passionately desires that everything that was lost by the first man, due to his embracing of sin and then through the generations that followed, would once again be restored to us. Through the sacrifice of Jesus, the last man under the Abrahamic covenant, once again, God's manifest presence is available to us. He wants to walk with us and talk with us. Jesus was not only sacrificed for our sins, and He not only received stripes for our healing, but He also had to go through His most desperate moment of losing God's presence when He cried out, "My God, my God, why have you forsaken me?" (Matthew 27:46, NIV). He was made a sacrifice for our sins and experienced separation from the Father in order to restore our relationship with Him. God's presence was restored to us.

God is omnipresent. He is present everywhere. His Spirit hovers over all. Yet not everyone gets to experience His presence in the way that is available to all. The veil of sin and ignorance separates us from Him until we receive the reconciliation that is available to all through the sacrifice of Jesus. In this, our sins are put away from us, and the Father welcomes us with open arms. We not only get to know *about* Him but also to know Him. His presence becomes available to us. Sadly, not even all Christians who have turned to God and believe in Him can say that they have experienced the tangible presence of God. So why is this important, and how do we experience His presence?

If our Christian lives are all about believing in God and knowing about Him from the Bible and in sermons, if it is all about going to church and doing good works, it becomes a religion to follow. Like the Pharisees of old, we become religious in our thinking and works, and this is the God we portray to the world. We may experience His goodness to us from time to time in answered prayer, but it is a random experience. We can even start to justify the bad experiences in between as the bad things that have come to us from God so we can learn important life lessons. In the in-between times, we are lost and act just like anybody else in the world who does not know Christ. In fact, if we are honest, we probably get more pleasure from going shopping or to the movies than in our experience with God. But the psalmist in Psalm 16:11, NIV, says, "you will fill me with joy in your presence, with eternal pleasures at your right hand." Surely, since God has not changed, this must be true for us today. How can that become our experience? How do we experience this presence of God that fills us with joy and eternal pleasure?

THE ONE THING

We all go to church for different reasons. Primarily, we go with an expectancy. What are we expecting? In some ways, we go for our needs to be fulfilled, to get relief from the pain in our hearts from broken relationships, to relieve anxiety about finances and our children, jobs, future, ill health, and to receive a word of encouragement to plod along on the path we're on. And that is wonderful. God's Word encourages us not to forsake the gathering with believers. There is such power in that. Yet, I am convinced that even while sitting in church, our hearts are crying for an encounter with the living God. The source of it all. The source of life. Pure, unadulterated, flow from the throne of God, containing in it everything we need.

What do we really need? Healing for our emotions, hope for our circumstances, forgiveness for our wrongs, grace to forgive those who have wronged us, and promises that our futures will be okay. Whatever we need is available to us in God's presence. When we start to flow with the Spirit of the living God, we have access to all these. But we receive none of these by striving for them.

> The only way we get to partake in all of God's blessings is through a place of restful believing and abiding in Him.

We have a God who is good. He is compassionate. He is kind. He loves us. He has a good plan for each one of our lives. He wants to help us in our times of need. He wants to draw us out of all the troubles we encounter in this world (Psalm 34:19). He wants to draw close to us. His presence is always available to us. "The Lord your God is in your midst, a mighty one who will save; he will rejoice over you with gladness; he will quiet you by his love; he will exult over you with loud singing" (Zephaniah 3:17, ESV). This is His desire for each one of us. He wants to quiet us with His love.

We live very busy lives in a very busy world. Oftentimes, our Christian lives get centered on busyness as well. We can become Marthas in our serving and doing and then complain about how much we are doing or maybe how some others are not. But if we want to experience God's presence, for seasons in our lives we must become Marys and learn to sit at the feet of Jesus and listen to Him. In rebuking Martha: "'Martha, Martha,' the Lord answered, 'you are worried and upset about many things, but few things are needed—or indeed only one. Mary has chosen what is better, and it will not be taken away from her'" (Luke 10:41–42, NIV). Notice that Jesus says few things are needed and then as if really wanting to make a point says, "or indeed only one." We need to do this through seasons of our lives and in fact as often as needed. Psalm 46:10, NIV, urges us to "Be still, and know that I am God; I will be exalted among the nations, I will be exalted in the earth." The art of being still is quite difficult for us in today's world. But if we are to experience God's tangible presence, we must learn it.

SOAKING IN HIS PRESENCE

It is invaluable that we read the Word, that we go to church, that we fellowship with other believers, that we give and serve, and do all the good things that we know to do. But none of these should take precedence over our times alone, basking in God's presence. We must be intentional to do this. Nothing else matters more. It is indeed the one thing that must not be taken away from us. We must each discover the tools that allow us this still time with the Lord. We must give ourselves permission to spend some quiet, undivided time with the Lord. We must get into the place of His presence and allow ourselves to marinate or "soak" in it.

In January 1994, revival broke out at a small church in Toronto, Canada, called the Toronto Airport Christian Fellowship or TACF, now called Catch the Fire Ministries, and God's manifest presence started to be experienced in power and glory. People were affected in huge ways and started to get saved, healed, and delivered. They found this one tool to be invaluable to the growth of a Christian seeking after God's heart, and it has been called "soaking" in God's presence. Literally it means posturing ourselves before God, focusing on Him, and then being still and just waiting on His presence. As we wait on Him, He is faithful and shows up, or rather once our souls are still enough and the loud chatter of this world and our minds starts to die down, we are able to key into His presence, which has always been there. We are able to hear His whispers and see what He wants to show us as the eyes of or spirits are opened up to Him.

Our heightened sensory awareness of His presence usually evokes some sensory responses in us. During these times, He is able to point to heart issues that are contrary to Him, and we must be radical to allow Him to deal with these, such as unforgiveness, judgments against ourselves and others, and any other sin that is not according to His heart. As long as we are open and willing, He helps us with our weaknesses (Romans 8:26). These can become powerful times of healing and restoration for us, and we learn to develop our relationship with the Father and receive from Him that which we have need of. His forgiveness, mercy, and grace are freely available to us.

It is this place of His presence where we are brought face-to-face with His glory. Our Christian experience is elevated from being a temporal and cerebral one, one that we can fully comprehend and explain, to one that is supernatural. This is where we have the fullness of true joy. This is the place where our souls are still enough that God is able to reach the deepest places in our hearts to draw out the dross, to restore, to heal, to set free and deliver, to give us answers, and to show us strategies. This is where it becomes possible to have even supernatural encounters. The ears and eyes of our spirit may be opened to see and encounter the King of kings, and we will never be the same again.

HIS PRESENCE GIVES US REST

Talking with Moses in Exodus 33:14, NIV, God tells him, "My Presence will go with you, and I will give you rest." That promise was not just for Moses. It is for us today. His presence gives us rest. We can know God, we can read the Word, we can go to church, and we can give and serve. Even when we have a relationship with God and others, even when we have faith and walk in freedom, we are brought into a deeper place of rest when we learn to recognize God's tangible presence and start to inhabit it. Just like His presence gave rest to Moses, it gives rest to us today.

> As we are diligent to inhabit the place of His presence, eventually we become the place of His dwelling and the carriers of His glorious presence.

We become those who reflect His glory. We become true sons and daughters created in His image and likeness. We become people after His heart the way He always intended. Will we say yes and pursue this calling? There is no greater rest. Rest in Him, soak in His spirit, then go out from that place and you will be transformed, you will have everything you need to face your giants, you will have God's own tangible presence with you.

Like David in Psalm 27:4, AMPC, may this become the cry of our hearts: "One thing have I asked of the Lord, that will I seek, inquire for, *and* [insistently] require: that I may dwell in the house of the Lord [in His presence] all the days of my life, to behold *and* gaze upon the beauty [the sweet attractiveness and the delightful loveliness] of the Lord and to meditate, consider, *and* inquire in His temple."

KEY 6:

LITERAL REST

GOD RESTS ON THE SEVENTH DAY

In following Christ, we are invited to a life where we can have literal rest in our lives besides the perpetual spiritual rest we have in the midst of pursuing our divine destinies. We see in the story of creation that after God completed the work of creation in six days, He then rested on the seventh day (Genesis 2:2). He consecrated the day and made it holy. He ceased from creating. It was all complete. It was all good. It was perfect. God's creation was flawless and beautiful. I doubt God was so exhausted He had to call all angels and declare a day of flopping in their resting places to recover from it. It must have been a holy moment.

I can imagine the angels rejoicing and worshiping and the sense of shalom or completeness to the beautiful creation. The sense of glory, wonder, and awe! The glorious One who created everything created man in His image and likeness (Genesis 1:27) to be an extension of His glory. His desire was for man to fill the earth and rule over creation (Genesis 1:26). This creation was meant to be an extension of Heaven, and man was to rule over it like God rules over Heaven. God's will was to be done on earth as it is in Heaven. God created man on the sixth day of creation and then ceased from the work of creation. Man was formed once the work of the rest of the creation had been completed. Man was formed on the sixth day, which was then succeeded by the sabbath, and he was placed in a finished glorious creation.

Man was to enjoy the splendor of creation and utilize his gifts to take care of and rule over it. God offered us a finished creation to rule over, and man was to "to tend and keep it" (Genesis 2:15, NKJV). It was only after Adam failed to fall in line with God's plan and sin made an entry into God's highest creation that the ground was cursed, and the result was thorns and thistles and man's charge became one of "painful toil" (Genesis 3:17, NIV). This is where most of us live, even today. Our work feels like painful toil; we wish for rest, we wish to slow down the pace of life, and we wish we didn't have to work so hard for our resources.

THE SABBATH COMMANDMENT

Once Israel was set apart to be a holy people of God to demonstrate the glory and power of God, they were given the Ten Commandments and then the Mosaic Law to govern them until "the Seed to whom the promise referred had come" (Galatians 3:19), referring to Jesus. One of the Ten Commandments given to man is the command to keep the sabbath. In its entirety, it reads: "Remember the Sabbath day by keeping it holy. Six days you shall labor and do all your work, but the seventh day is a sabbath to the Lord your God. On it you shall not do any work, neither you, nor your son or daughter, nor your male or female servant, nor your animals, nor any foreigner residing in your towns. For in six days the Lord made the heavens and the earth, the sea, and all that is in them, but he rested on the seventh day. Therefore the Lord blessed the Sabbath day and made it holy" (Exodus 20:8–11, NIV).

So how does sabbath apply to us today? Does God require us to take a day off for the sole purpose of worshipping Him and for rest? Is this to be a day of inactivity?

So many of us have this conflict. We want to and feel like we need to take a day off to rest and to go to church. But what about kid's games and sports? What about the lawn that needs to be mowed and the dishes that need to be done? How about the preparation that is required for return to work the next day? How do we navigate these things on our day of rest? Since Jesus is our forerunner, first let's look at the life of Jesus and see how He followed the law, and especially how He kept the sabbath.

Jesus was a Jew, and so the expectation was that He follow the Jewish Law. Jesus stated very clearly in Matthew 5:17, NIV, "Do not think that I have come to abolish the Law or the Prophets; I have not come to abolish them but to fulfill them." However, from the stories in the Bible, it seems that during His life on earth, Jesus continuously defied the religious people of that time. He was critical of them. He did not speak against the law but against the exacting religious leaders who had become harsh in their expectation of people to follow the law. He criticized how they "crush people with unbearable religious demands and never lift a finger to ease the burden" (Matthew 23:4, NLT). What was meant for good had been turned into something oppressive. In Matthew 5:7, in the Sermon on the Mount, Jesus teaches His followers very clearly that the old rules and even the Ten Commandments were inadequate unless they involved a genuine change of heart. Jesus raises the bar of Old Testament law.

In the Sermon on the Mount, talking to His disciples and followers, Jesus makes it very clear that the commands of God are not in the outward actions alone but that God is concerned with what's happening in our hearts. Through His life and death, He became the fulfillment of the law and paved the way for man to walk in relationship with God. What the law was unable to do because of its high standard and man's sinful nature, now became possible. He clearly demonstrated and spoke about how to fulfill the law. So how does this specifically apply to the keeping of the sabbath?

HOW DID JESUS KEEP THE SABBATH?

Let us look at the life of Jesus to see how He kept the sabbath. Matthew 12:1–8 describes the story when Jesus was walking through grain fields along with His disciples on a sabbath day and they began to pick some heads of grain. The Pharisees were not happy about this and questioned Jesus saying what they were doing was "unlawful on the Sabbath." Jesus in His wisdom narrated to them the story of David and his companions from an incident when they "were hungry" and he entered the house of God, ate the consecrated bread, and shared with his companions as well. Typically, this bread was "only for the priests." Jesus said this as in justification being above legalism.

What David did was in the Old testament Times, in the times where the law was to be revered, and yet Jesus presented this incident as a parallel to justify His disciples picking and eating grains of corn on the sabbath. He admonishes them by saying, "If you had known what these words mean, 'I desire mercy, not sacrifice,' you would not have condemned the innocent. For the Son of Man is Lord of the Sabbath." Jesus places a higher value on mercy and resulting life than the blind following of tenets, if that resulted in placing a higher premium on sacrifice than life and mercy. Jesus came that we may have "life and have it to the full"[1] (John 10:10, NIV). Jesus did not come to abolish the law but to show a way that is higher, a way of mercy and justice and fullness of life. Jesus proclaims Himself Lord of the sabbath. In Him, the righteous requirement of the law is fulfilled. In Mark 2:27–28, He says "The Sabbath was made for man, not man for the Sabbath. So the Son of Man is Lord even of the

Sabbath."[2] Clearly, the sabbath rest is created for man, not a legalistic requirement of the law.

There are seven documented miracles Jesus did on the sabbath. In John 5, when He is questioned about the miracle of healing the man who sat by the pool near the sheep gate, He responded: "My Father is still working, and I am working also."[3] When the religious people started to prosecute him, in His response He said in John 5:19, "Very truly I tell you, the Son can do nothing by himself; he can do only what he sees his Father doing, because whatever the Father does the Son also does."[4] Clearly, Jesus was doing the will of the Father, once again demonstrating that the Father's will is always life and liberty. God did not mean for the sabbath to be a day of inactivity but a day when His will was done if it involved life and good works.

> Clearly, His sabbath and ours is to do the will of the Father because in that there is rest.

PURPOSE OF THE SABBATH

In keeping the sabbath, there is a sense of cessation from our works and entering into God's rest. As we cease from our labors and enter into God's rest, there is not only rest in the spiritual sense, but this rest translates to every aspect of our lives. I don't believe the sabbath was meant to be a day for us to be idle, lay in bed all day watching Netflix. The purpose of the sabbath then is to give us life and a renewed awe and wonder of God and His creation. It is a celebration of life and should be a joyful day of rest. However, if this rest then becomes a law unto us that in turn becomes a bondage and removes the liberty to choose/participate with acts producing life, then it defies the purpose for which it was given to mankind. I think this becomes a day for us to enjoy the fruits of our labors from the week, to spend literal time resting. And if something comes our way that pertains to life, just like the other commands God gives us, it for each one to live it out with God. Make practical adjustments to your life to make this a restful day for your family to attend church, but by all means remember that the sabbath is made for us, not us for the sabbath, and just like Jesus we live it out with God at the center as we aspire to do His will.

In Colossians 2:16–17, NIV, Paul in addressing the church in Colossae, admonishes them saying "do not let anyone judge you by what you eat or drink, or with regard to a religious festival, a New Moon celebration or a Sabbath day." These are a shadow of the things that were to come; the reality, however, is found in Christ. In speaking to the Romans on the same theme, he repeats in a similar vein. He says in Romans 14:5–6, NIV, "One person considers one day more sacred than another; another considers every day alike. Each of them should be fully convinced in their own mind. Whoever regards one day as special does so to the Lord." It is clear that Jesus gives us the freedom to attend church on Saturday or Sunday. And if our work requires us to work on Sunday, attend sports with our kids, or take care of other business, God does not condemn us by any means.

THE NEED FOR LITERAL REST

That does not discount the need for actual literal rest. Jesus Himself who was in constant communion with God, His heavenly Father, needed to get away with His disciples and on His own to rest and to pray. Mark 6:31 tells us that because so many people were coming and going that they did not even have a chance to eat. He said to them, "Come with me by yourselves to a quiet place and get some rest."[5] In Luke 6:12, NIV, we are told that "One of those days Jesus went out to a mountainside to pray, and spent the night praying to God." Jesus not only took time to rest and pray, but the famous story of Mary and Martha well illustrates that busyness is not necessarily the part that God desires for us. There are times when we need to just get away.

Jesus illustrates this in His response to Martha when she complains about Mary not helping her with hospitality. "'Martha, Martha,' the Lord answered, 'you are worried and upset about many things, but few things are needed—or indeed only one. Mary has chosen what is better, and it will not be taken away from her'"[6] (Luke 10:41–42, NIV).

Work is not an option. We were not created to lead an idle life. Let's look at the parable of the talents in Matthew 25:13–30, where a man about to go on a journey calls three of his slaves and entrusts them with five, two, and one talent each. The talent referred to in this story was a fairly large amount of wealth.[7] The parable goes on to tell us that the slave who was entrusted with five talents went and traded with them and gained five more talents. Similarly, the man who had received two talents gained two more. But the man who received the one talent went away, dug a hole in the ground, and hid his master's money. When the master returned, the two slaves who had multiplied the talents were acknowledged for their faithfulness and put in charge of many things. The slave who had hidden the talent that was entrusted to him out of fear, lost even what he had, and it was handed to the other slaves. In fact, he was dealt with harshness with the master calling him lazy and wicked.

Literally we all have abilities we are to use. We have all heard the quote: use it or lose it. This parable clearly teaches us that we are all meant to live highly creative lives and use our gifts and talents to be highly productive people. We are meant to multiply and do great exploits for God in the area of our gifts and talents. But in the midst of it, we must make time to sit at the feet of Jesus, read the Word, and develop our intimacy with God. In fact, if we don't, we will eventually lose our Christ-centered focus and become "work" focused, which is where a lot of Christians are. We work at work, we work at home, we work at church, and we long for rest. Like Martha, we are worried and upset by many things, but in our hearts, we long for the rest of Mary.

WASTED EFFORT

Psalm 127:1–2 gives us an understanding of the wasted effort in toiling for something that does not originate from the heart of God. "Unless the Lord builds the house, those who build it labor in vain. Unless the Lord guards the city, the watchman stays awake in vain. It is in vain that you rise up early and go late to rest, eating the bread of anxious toil; for he gives to his beloved sleep."[8] In 1 Corinthians 3:10–15, Paul is speaking to the Corinthians about their efforts at building the church and urges them to build with care. And because their work would be shown for what it is, that it would be revealed with fire, the fire would test the quality of each person's work and would either be rewarded or burnt up. The Holy Spirit says the same to us today. Why struggle and toil for something that is not of the Lord? Why toil for something that will not stand the test of eternity? The Lord invites us to come to a place of rest in Him, make that our habitation, and do all things from that place. There is eternal reward when our plans flow from the heart of God and fulfil His purpose. That is a life of blessed rest.

There is rest when God is in our plans and efforts.

"In all your ways submit to him, and he will make your paths straight"[9] (Proverbs 3:6, NIV). God is interested in every detail of your life. He is passionate to keep you on the path of your divine calling and blessing. Learn to recognize His voice and do as He says. Do not get yourself entangled in pursuits that simply drain your time, energy, or resources. Proverbs 3:21–24 urges us to "not let wisdom and understanding out of your sight, preserve sound judgment and discretion; they will be life for you, an ornament to grace your neck. Then you will go on your way in safety, and your foot will not stumble. When you lie down, you will not be afraid; when you lie down, your sleep will be sweet."[10] That is the kind of rest God desires for us.

We must first believe this and then make room for Him to come through for us. In all your actions, keep pleasing God as your only compass, and you will not fail. This will eliminate wasted efforts to try to please people or pursue plans that are not of Him. When you live this way, He will certainly lead you along restful ways so you can say, just like the psalmist "He makes me lie down in green pastures, he leads me beside quiet waters, he refreshes my soul. He guides me along the right paths for his name's sake."[11] (Psalm 23:2–3, NIV). In seasons of our life, we might have to wait patiently for Him, but be assured He hears your prayers. "Be still before the Lord and wait patiently for him"[12] (Psalm 37:7). There are many battles we do not need to fight. The Lord is with us and fights them for us.

If you find yourself in the midst of painful toil, know that there is a better way. Step back and step into God's purposes. We are to tend and keep what He has given us. He will surely show you the way and direct your steps. Our only striving should be to enter into the rest we are offered.

KEY 7:

MANIFESTING CHRIST

WHAT ARE YOU MANIFESTING?

In the twenty-first century, with all the advancements in technology, medicine, communication, etc., God is often considered a "maybe figure" for the religious-minded people. How much more difficult is it for people to wrap their minds around the concept of man being created in God's image? In a world where man has accomplished great feats and thrives on 24/7 internet, where space travel seems to have become inevitable, and genome modifications are possible, we have learned to live without God, or so we think. In daily lives marked with all our fabulous accomplishments, people don't have time to ponder over questions related to God. We hear news of the awesome, the good, the bad, and the ugly people making this world what it is, and it becomes easier for people to believe in possible alien existence than to see the reality of God in the midst of such chaos. Why should we even believe that there is a God, and more so, believe that God created man in His image? It is perhaps a fable to most.

What do we display? We manifest who we are through demonstration. Every part of our being adds up to "display or show (a quality or feeling) by one's acts or appearance."[1] We impact our atmosphere and those around us in how we manifest in seen and unseen ways, for good or bad. We human beings are complex, to say the least. We can also cover our true selves with pretense and a false manifestation of who we are, how we are feeling, and our actions. Take a moment to check yourself. What are you displaying? What are you thinking, feeling, judging, saying? How are you acting? How are you living? Who are your friends? What do you do for a living? How do you take care of yourself? How do you treat others? How do you spend your time? Our bodies display the sum of our genetic makeup, our diet, our exercise, and our age. Our behavior and what we say is the sum total of our beliefs, our upbringing, influences of our environment, our makeup, and personalities. The deep person within us expresses outwardly or sometimes fakes it. We cannot possibly name all the things that make us who we are. But we manifest in our physical appearance, with our words and actions, all of who we are.

DO CHRISTIANS DISPLAY GOD?

So, if we as Christians have invited God through His Holy Spirit to live in us, do we look and act like Him? Most of us, even those of us who have invited Him into our hearts and lives, would be hesitant to say we are truly displaying God in us and through us. Why is that so? Did God create us in His image and likeness and then just leave us alone to struggle as lost people constantly in need, constantly battling things in our lives, and our relationship with God predominantly resting in desperate pleas for God to hear our prayers, meet our needs, and allay our anxieties? It is impossible for a Christian who is anxious about life, self-seeking for His needs, or trying to serve God in his flesh to manifest God. Yes, we must be honest about where we are in our Christian walk, and He wants to hear about our needs and anxieties. Yes, He rewards our attempts to serve Him. However, that's a pitiful expression of a God who is all powerful, all sufficient, all able! Until we know God, until we develop a relationship with Him, until we start to trust Him and His Word for us, until we start to believe and receive all that He has for us, until we ourselves are settled in our souls, we cannot start to grow in our God nature and manifest it to those around us.

In fact, a look through the Bible clearly reveals that through history even God's elect and those who loved God, and even did great exploits for God, were not really Godlike. Adam and Eve had to leave the Garden of Eden. In Noah's time, sin had become so pervasive that God caused a great flood to wipe out humanity. At the tower of Babel, humanity was scattered to contain sin and defiance. Even Abraham with whom God was greatly pleased due to His faith has been documented to lie about his wife to protect himself, and he introduced her as his sister. David the king, who wrote many of the famous psalms to praise God, committed adultery with Bathsheba and later strategized the killing of her husband. Yes, they loved God, but their actions were certainly not Godlike. So how does the whole "God made man in His image and likeness" thing play out? Is that still true, or was that just for the first man and woman?

The Bible tells us that God created man, "in our image, in our likeness" (Genesis 1:26, NIV) to rule over creation with Him. He was to be an extension of God's glory. He was to exhibit the divine attributes of God and be to Earth what God is to Heaven. Due to man's embracing of sin, he was unable to walk in God's calling. He was not able to rule over creation as God had intended. He was separated from God, and death became his portion. For generations, God tried to call out a small group of people to be His people, to follow His command, and live blameless lives. Due to their lack of faith and inability to follow God's commands, man continued to walk away from God's intention for him. God's image and likeness was not manifested.

WAS JESUS GOD?

In John 14:8, NIV, when the disciples of Jesus asked Him to show them God, saying, "that will be enough for us," Jesus's response was that anyone who had seen Him had seen God. Jesus came in flesh like that of sinful man, lived a sinless life, and satisfied the law. He exhibited God in every way. That is why the Bible says in Hebrews 1:3, NLT, "The Son radiates God's own glory and expresses the very character of God." In John 5:19, Jesus also says that he did nothing by Himself and only did what He saw the Father doing. His actions were completely

Godlike. Not only did he exhibit the glory of God in every way, despite being in human flesh, through His sacrifice on behalf of our sins, the Bible then tells us that, "When he had cleansed us from our sins, he sat down in the place of honor at the right hand of the majestic God in heaven" (Hebrews 1:3, NLT). The way was made for sinful humanity to once again be restored to a sinless state in accepting the sacrifice of Jesus and embracing our union with the Father.

The Bible tells us that "he who is joined to the Lord becomes one spirit with him" (1 Corinthians 6:17, ESV). When Jesus was having the proverbial Last Supper with His disciples, He told them that once He was gone, the Father would send them the Holy Spirit who would come to live within them and would never leave them. The Holy Spirit sent to reside in us enables us to be everything God has called us to be. We are to rise up to become those who are restored to being His image bearers and carriers of His glory. We are to become His many sons and daughters of whom Christ is the forerunner. Jesus also tells them that "whoever believes in me will do the works I have been doing, and they will do even greater things than these" (John 14:12, NIV).

In 1 John 4:17, TPT, we are told that "By *living in God*, love has been brought to its full expression in us so that we may fearlessly face the day of judgment, because all that Jesus now is, so are we in this world." So, we are to be in this world all of what Jesus was. What was Jesus to the world? Countercultural, counteroppressive religion, teacher, healer, miracle worker, the very image and nature of God. Jesus Himself says that He did what He saw the Father doing and said what He heard the Father saying. He calls Himself the image of God. He tells His disciples that if they have seen Him, they have seen the Father. And we are to be like Him, be like the Father, which is no surprise. We are created in the image and likeness of God! And the way has been paved for us to walk in this.

MANIFESTING HIM

The great I AM dwells in us, once invited. And we are to become those who demonstrate Him in us and through us. We are to be the light of the world. We are to be the salt of the world. We are to make Him known through our good deeds. We are to manifest His glory, to make it known. Once He comes to dwell in us, we cannot say that we are sick, we are weak, and we are not able. We are to speak what He is in us, and through Him we are able, we are whole, we are hopeful, and we are okay. Our greatest joy and delight and rest is when we are so one with the Father, so led of the Holy Spirit that we can truly say we have been crucified with Christ, and it is no longer we who live, but Christ lives in us. The life we now live in the body, we live by faith in the Son of God, who loves us and gave Himself for us (Galatians 2:20). This is where we are free from the shackles of sin and self.

We are indeed free to follow Christ. We are free from all things that keep us from being able to hear God's voice, think God thoughts, and live like Christ. Indeed "in this world we are like Jesus" (1 John 4:17, NIV). We are not of the world, just as Jesus was not (John 17:16). We see and have risen to our identities as sons and daughters of God. We recognize that "God raised us up with Christ and seated us with him in the heavenly realms in Christ Jesus" (Ephesians 2:6, NIV). We become carriers of His presence and glory. God does not ask us for the impossible. After all, we have the mind of Christ and we are the body of Christ. Should not His people who have the mind, body, and spirit of Christ, who was the image of God, not walk as Jesus Himself did? The Holy Spirit enables us to exhibit the virtues of Christ or the fruit of the Holy Spirit. Our creativity and individual gifts and calling are to enable us to function together as the body of Christ and together become in this world as He was.

THE PROCESS AND JOURNEY

This change is not instantaneous. We embrace the process and journey. We embrace the cross that nullifies our pitiful souls, that struggle along in this life, and daily offers us a glimpse into the magic Kingdom of God where only beauty exists. Once we are His and He is ours, it starts the beautiful journey where we are forgiven, where we are able to forgive others, where there is hope beyond the grave, where all things become possible, where our limited finite selves are now able to draw from the vast expanse of His infinite Kingdom and grow until we start to believe like Him, think like Him, and act like Him.

Daily we forfeit our weakness for His strength, our sadness for His joy, our hopelessness for His hope, our sickness for His wholeness, our busyness for His rest.

Above all, we manifest love, which is His ultimate expression. We cannot do this as long as we are worried, anxious, and absorbed with our problems. We have to truly come to a place where we can say, "God has me in the palm of His hand." We do not worry because He cares for us. We are not self-seeking, proud, or boastful because the Holy Spirit enables us to be so. When we encounter problems, we remind ourselves that all things will work together for our good, which includes the problem at hand. In fierce storms, we know that Jesus the overcomer is in the boat with us. In insurmountable difficulties and blockades, we know that He will bring us out of them. Our situations and difficulties are not our focus. We walk in freedom and love. We are free to manifest Christ. We are free to love the Lord our God with all of our soul, strength, and might, and we are able to love our neighbors as ourselves. We become conduits for His presence, the One who is wisdom, healing, and everything this world needs. Above all, He is love, and we are to manifest Him.

REST AND MANIFEST

> When we are in relationship with Him,
> When we are confident in our identity of who we are,
> When we are so rooted and grounded in our faith that we are always believing for the impossible,
> When we walk in the true freedom that Christ purchased for us,
> When we become carriers of His presence,

When we cease to struggle in our strength and
start to manifest Him, who above all is love,
We have come to a place of unshakable,
unspeakable, overwhelming rest.
This is the rest God offers us.

We are all invited. He says, "Come to me, all you who are weary and burdened, and I will give you rest" (Matthew 11:28, NIV). Are we manifesting such deep, wonderful, tangible rest that we carry it wherever we go, whatever we do?

CONCLUSION

It seems to me we are all seeking and searching for more in our lives, even in our quest to find God or to advance His Kingdom. Yes, all that is good. But if all of our lives are about seeking, searching, and doing, ultimately how do we ever find rest?

This is what I hear God's Spirit tell me:

> *Seek Me, find Me, find your satisfaction in Me. I am always there with you and for you. Feel My embrace in My presence. Learn to live with Me. Find your satisfaction in Me. Find your value and worth in Me. Do not burden others, even your own parents, spouses, or children, with ascribing worth to you. Know that your worth is inherent because I put it in you.*
>
> *If you make a mistake, be quick to repent and receive forgiveness; the price has been paid for all your sins. It*

is a gift. Be quick to walk in this gift. In the same way, see others as God sees them and be quick to forgive as He forgives you. Forgive everyone who has ever wronged you. Know that I am enough for you, and I am able to bring justice to all situations.

Don't worry. Know that I am your provider. I will provide. Do not be slothful, however. Keep your feet moving and hands busy. I have given each one gifts and talents. Use these, and you will never run out of provision. When sickness attacks you, know that I am the healer. Trust me for your healing. Do what you know to do in the natural, and I will do only what I can do in the supernatural.

Love your families. Love your spouses and children with extravagant love. Honor and care for the elderly, weak, and feeble. Give alms and charity to the poor. Feed the hungry. Care for the homeless. Love your pets. Be kind to animals. Decorate your homes. Take care of your bodies. Nurture nature. See the beauty around you. Develop the awareness, and you will see My hand at work all around you.

See Me in the moment, and you will know which way to go, what to do, and what to say. Be in tune with My voice though, and be ready to step into action as I show you the way and what to do. Be flexible to move as you hear My voice. Stop when I ask you to. Know that I am always with you. In that, find rest.

Be naturally supernatural, but then learn to be supernaturally natural so you can live the life I created you for. Gather others to Me so they may also know the love of the Father. Above all, find My love and then go and give it out. A genuine extravagant love. In Me, find your joy, and you will never run out. Learn to rest in Me....

In this world, you have to strive for all things. In the Kingdom of God, you receive all things by ultimately resting in Him.

ABOUT THE AUTHOR

Sunita Ahuja is an ordained minister who works as a physical therapist and considers it a platform for reaching her world with the love and healing hands of Christ. Her life's passion is to walk in love, to serve those around her, and do what God wants her to do daily. She has a passion to share the love, joy, and rest of Christ with those around her and a deep desire to see all walk in their divine calling.

In recent years, God has taken her on a journey and given her revelation regarding His perspective on rest and the seven keys to living a life saturated with rest. Sunita now has a passionate desire to enable others to walk in it. She wants to share with others how they can come to that beautiful place of supernatural rest in their lives and walk it out daily. Sunita lives in Virginia, with her husband and three children.

ENDNOTES

INTRODUCTION

1. Psalm 34:19, NIV

CHAPTER 2

1. https://biblehub.com/hebrew/5117.htm
2. https://en.wikibooks.org/wiki/Hebrew_Roots/
   Neglected_Commandments/Sabbath/Apologetics/Purpose
3. https://biblehub.com/greek/373.htm
4. https://biblehub.com/hebrew/5117.htm

CHAPTER 3

1. https://www.mentalfloss.com/article/12500/11-historical-geniuses-and-their-possible-mental-disorders
2. https://www.theatlantic.com/health/archive/2012/09/historical-geniuses-and-their-psychiatric-conditions/262249/

KEY 3

1. Google, "faith," accessed April 27, 2020, https://www.google.com/search?q=definition+of+faith&rlz=1C1CHBF_enUS864US866&oq=definition+of+faith&aqs=chrome..69i57j0l7.11022j1j7&sourceid=chrome&ie=UTF-8.

KEY 5

1. https://blog.israelbiblicalstudies.com/jewish-studies/glory-mean-hebrew-insights-dr-eli/
2. Ibid

KEY 6

1. John 10:10, NIV
2. Mark 2:27–28, NIV
3. John 5:17, CSB, https://www.biblestudytools.com/csb/john/5-17.html
4. John 5:19, NIV
5. Mark 6:31, NIV
6. Luke 10:41–42

7. https://en.wikipedia.org/wiki/Talent_(measurement)
8. Psalm 127:1–2, ESV
9. Proverbs 3:6, NIV
10. Proverbs 3:21–24, NIV
11. Psalm 23:2–3, NIV
12. Psalm 37:7, NIV

KEY 7

1. Google, "manifest," accessed April 27, 2020,
   https://www.google.com/search?q=manifest
   +meaning&rlz=1C1CHBF_enUS864US866
   &oq=manifest+&aqs=chrome.6.69i57j0l6j69i61
   .11589j0j7&sourceid=chrome&ie=UTF-8

www.ingramcontent.com/pod-product-compliance
Lightning Source LLC
LaVergne TN
LVHW051415080426
835508LV00022B/3097